PUMPED

Confidence techniques that will have you
standing taller in the world

Jodie Bruce-Clarke

Copyright © 2015 Jodie Bruce-Clarke

All rights reserved. No part of this publication may be reproduced, stored in a retrieval system or transmitted in any form or by any means, electronic, mechanical, photocopying, recording or otherwise, without the prior written permission of the publisher.

The information, views, opinions and visuals expressed in this publication are solely those of the author(s) and do not reflect those of the publisher. The publisher disclaims any liabilities or responsibilities whatsoever for any damages, libel or liabilities arising directly or indirectly from the contents of this publication.

The author of this book does not dispense medical advice or prescribe the use of any technique as a form of treatment for physical, emotional, or medical problems without the advice of a physician, either directly or indirectly. The intent of the author is only to offer information of a general nature to help you in your quest for emotional well-being and good health. In the event you use any of the information in this book for yourself, which is your constitutional right, the author and the publisher assume no responsibility for your actions.

A copy of this publication can be found in the National Library of Australia.

Some names and identifying details have been changed to protect the privacy of individuals.

ISBN: 978-0-9941889-0-8 (pbk.)

Published by Rise Women

www.RiseWomen.com

Dedication

*For the precious gifts of life, love, belief and confidence,
I dedicate this book to my mother.
You are the light that I follow every day.*

CONTENTS

COME ON UP THE VIEW IS INCREDIBLE
Authors note

PART 1
HEELS ON, STAND UP!
Changing Your Thoughts and Attitudes to
Live a Confident Woman's Life

YOUR MOMENT OF TRUTH

ONE
FINDING LITTLE MISS CONFIDENCE
29
What is Confidence? Blowing Open the Myths!
Laying the Foundation

TWO
ACCEPTANCE
THE KEY TO AN UNSHAKEABLE FOUNDATION OF CONFIDENCE
41
Accepting You
Acceptance of your Past
Acceptance of Others
Acceptance of Circumstances

THREE
FEEL FEAR? WELCOME TO THE HUMAN RACE
75
How to See Fear Differently

FOUR
JUST GIVE IT UP
BREAKING THE CHAINS THAT BIND YOU
89
Give up Blame of Yourself and Others
Give up the Past

Give up Listening to Self-doubt
Give up Gossip
Give up Internal Criticism
Give up External Criticism
Give up Excuses
Give up the Guilt

FIVE
RESPONSIBILITY
109
Seeing Responsibility Differently
Responsibility for your Commitments
Responsibility for your Negative Chatterbox
Responsibility for what comes out of your Mouth
Responsibility for your Mood
Responsibility for your Perception

SIX
IT'S ALL AN ILLUSION
127
The Illusion of the Wrong Decision
The Illusion of Reality
The Illusion of Failure
The Crystal Ball Factor

SEVEN
3 CLICKS AND YOU'RE HOME
145
Never Give In
No Low Flying Ducks

PART 2
GET PUMPED! BE CONFIDENT!
Designing Your Own Personal Confidence Program

THINK CONFIDENTLY
157
Acknowledgement Diary
WOW Book
Affirmations
Eliminate Self-Hate Behaviours

Manage Fear
In My Opinion
Ditch the Disempowering Thoughts
Worry Less About What Others Think

ACT CONFIDENTLY
175

Fake It Till You Make It
Find a Confident Woman as a Role Model
Confident Body Language
Bad Hair Days
Red Shoes, Red Bra's and All That's In-Between
Virtual Beauty
Body Image
Make Decisions
Be Self-Expressed
Set Achievable Inspiring Goals

LIVE CONFIDENTLY
203

Confidence is Catching
Surround Yourself
Confidence Buddy
Your Theme Song
Surround Yourself with Inspiration
Volunteer, Donate or Help
Focus on BIG Problems
Give a Compliment a Day
Set Up Your Environment for Success

THE DREAM

MY ATTITUDE OF GRATITUDE

ABOUT RISE WOMEN

Sugar and spice and all things nice. Really? What about strength, courage, compassion, tenacity, brains, grit, loyalty and confidence? That's what we're actually made of!

Come on up. The view is incredible!

It is no accident that I am writing a book about confidence. Looking back at my life, it seems the journey I am now on was inevitable.

In 2001, feeling as though I was caught in a rut, I hired a life coach and found that this process made me truly accountable for how my life was turning out. I was more motivated and inspired about what I could create for my life than ever before and, having recognised the incredible power of coaching, realised this was the path I simply had to follow.

I had always wanted to work with women, inspiring them to really take on their lives and go after their dreams; to move through the drama and to release the pain and guilt. So, later that year I took a leap of faith, trained to be a life coach and started my own business.

By the end of 2001 I had walked out of my life in the corporate world, set up a home office, bought myself a computer, printed some business cards and was officially open for business. The dream of building my own empire had begun (slowly but surely)!

If you have ever taken on the wonderful world of small business, you'll understand me when I say that those were some of the hardest months of my life. However, I was working with the most amazing clients who were committed to creating what they wanted in their lives, and the fulfilment I gained from guiding them was a reward that far outweighed the challenges I was facing.

The months rolled on and I started to see a pattern emerging. No matter what my clients' lives were about – I met business owners, housewives, young women, mortgage brokers, executives, students, mature women facing life changes and even a stripper – the common link between them was their lack of confidence. These intelligent, courageous and successful individuals were being utterly defeated by their lack of self-belief. It just didn't make sense.

Even more surprising to me was the fact that my clients didn't think their confidence was something they could really have an impact on. It became clear to me that many people struggle with confidence and are living with very little sense of self-belief most of the time. From experience, I *knew* there were ways to improve confidence levels and to find the internal freedom to create anything we want for our lives.

What also fascinated me was how people related to confidence. Consistently, I would hear clients, friends and business contacts say to me, 'Well it's all right for you, you've got confidence. I couldn't do that.' It was as though they were suggesting I had some special gift; that I had been born with a unique genetic code that lent itself to a confidence advantage they would never have.

Now, let's get this straight: I was not born with truckloads of confidence, I wasn't bestowed with a magical gift and my genetic code is pretty normal (debatable, I'm sure). Confidence has been something I have worked on daily. Over the years I have, quite unconsciously, developed my own personal confidence program and built it into my life. This program maintains my confidence at particular levels depending on where I need it to be. I have some techniques I use regularly that allow me to face those everyday challenges, and others I use when I need an instant burst of confidence or I'm about to do something way outside my comfort zone.

Hadn't everyone been using the same techniques? It seems not. You see, as young girls we are taught to eat with our mouths closed, sit up straight and even execute the intricacies of long division. Who teaches us how to maintain high levels of confidence, to feel good about ourselves and to see fear for what it really is? Nobody!

Come on up. The view is incredible!

So, I began explaining to my clients the techniques I used and helped them to design their own personalised confidence programs. This is how my business 'RiSe Women' was born. I wanted to blow open this concept of confidence and show individuals that they too can have the self-belief they have always envied in others. They too could lay a foundation of confidence in their lives – a foundation from which they can 'Rise' - by designing for themselves a confidence program and using the techniques.

Throughout my coaching practice, I see dramatic changes in each and every client once a confidence program has been employed. No matter what the goals - a new career, finding a relationship, weight loss or a finance shake-up – laying a strong foundation of confidence is always the first vital aspect required to take action. Then the rest starts to fall into place.

So how did I come to know about foundations of confidence? It is only now that I realise what an incredible influence my mother was on me when I was growing up.

During my teenage years, my mother was under intense pressure. She was a woman coping with a divorce, 3 children and the obligation to return to the workforce for the first time in 15 years. I watched her deal with a brain tumour diagnosis, struggle financially, and be forced to move us from the large family home to a small house that required enormous amounts of work. Mum moved through all these trials with awe-inspiring strength and determination. She increased her work skills and secured herself a job, removed the stress and resentment from her life to halt the tumour growth, fully renovated our home and continued to support her children financially and emotionally throughout.

It is now clear to me that she managed all of these factors so successfully by building herself a program of confidence. She read inspiring books, changed negative beliefs about herself, widened her perspective and took full responsibility for the way things were in her life. She came to understand the power of her thoughts and what it takes to fully accept who she was, her circumstances and how she saw others around her.

My mother's insights about confidence were instilled in me from these early teenage years. I had a person in my life that was a true role model, demonstrating the idea that I could have anything I wanted; that nothing was beyond my grasp. I was taught that achieving my dreams meant putting my mind to it, believing I could do it and getting into action. It was really that simple. Uniquely, it wasn't just words. I learnt because she lived it and I lived it with her.

There is no doubt that my mother moulded my view of the world in a powerfully positive way. Although I still feel fear, still question myself and still have doubts, I have a fixed underlying belief system forever reminding me that I can create anything I want. The trick is seeing the hurdles as just those, hurdles – and I am happy to say that I still view the world with the idea that no hurdle is insurmountable.

In 2006 I married and by 2007 I held my first child in my arms. She was beautiful, amazing and hungry – no one told me about having to breastfeed every 3 hours. It was such a massive life change for me! The very new journey of motherhood began and there was so much to learn, so many new mums to meet and a whole new realm of mother guilt feelings to contend with. Wow – now *they* carry some serious punch!

I decided to put my coaching and speaking (and ultimately my dream business) on hold so I could settle into motherhood. I worked part-time from home for a virtual training company and also set up another small business with a friend. Now, more than ever, I needed to work my confidence program as I settled into my brand new life with brand new challenges.

After my son was born in 2009 I struggled emotionally and had severe anxiety until, almost 12 months later, I was diagnosed with post-natal depression. A mild form, thank goodness, but nevertheless a challenging time. Although I had a very nice and comfortable life by conventional standards, I still felt quite unfulfilled. I was off-purpose and my increasing age was worrying me more by the minute. When would I get back to following my dream? Was I running out of time? Had I missed my chance? With young children in tow and working my part-time roles, I really couldn't see a way to bring my dreams back to life. I had lost my spark, lost my vision and ultimately lost my confidence in ever being able to make this dream come true.

It was this lack of self-belief that led me to doubt myself in many other areas of my life as well. I was constantly questioning whether I was a good mother, whether I was damaging my relationship and whether my family would be better off without me. I had taken on more responsibility in my part-time role, which had thrown my entire life into disarray. I couldn't sleep, had no energy, enthusiasm or motivation. And what was worse, I couldn't see a way out.

The turning point was when I met an old friend for coffee and launched into a very honest update about my life and my emotional state. He stopped me mid-sentence and said 'Jodie, can't you hear that?' He looked me straight in the eyes and said, 'Jodie, the alarm bells are ringing and you are not listening.' He was right. The alarms were ringing loud and clear. My life was spiralling out of control and I was not doing anything to stop it.

It was then that I realised what was important for me was to focus on my emotional health and get my confidence back on track. Over the next few years I made dramatic changes to all areas of my life. I resigned from my job, took positive steps to repair my mental and physical health and, once again, pulled out my ever-reliable confidence techniques.

It took time but slowly I was starting to feel like Jodie again. The spark, the vision and the confidence I'd lost were back. I knew that I was rebuilding my foundation – the foundation from which I could rise above the challenges of my past, and create my future.

And so, RiSe Women was reborn. I approached my good friend Anastasia, the stars aligned, the opportunity to work together presented itself and we both jumped at the chance.

Which brings me to this point of my journey; releasing a book in order to share my journey with other women, along with the most high-impact confidence boosters I know. The belief I now have in myself is allowing me to create the life I want. My goal is to help others understand the malleability and power of confidence by guiding them, supporting them and inspiring them to have the confidence levels they have always dreamed of. To help them achieve a level of confidence that gives them a life where they are free to follow their passions, create their dreams and allow the truest expression of themselves to flow before us. A level of confidence that inspires the women around them, teaches their daughters to be confident and gives them the power to stand up and make a bigger contribution to the world.

Everyone deserves that level of confidence at their fingertips!

So, turn the page and warn your friends…supreme confidence awaits!

Free Workbook

To obtain your free, downloadable workbook that accompanies this book, go to
www.RiseWomen.com/pumped_workbook/

Confidence is worth every minute of the energy you put into achieving it.

PART 1

Heels on, Stand Up!

Changing your thoughts and attitudes to live
a Confident Woman's life

Your Moment of Truth

So, this is it! Firstly, as a woman who is reading this book to increase her confidence, I want to acknowledge you. That small act indicates a quest for more of this deliciously rich world, and I'm thrilled to be working with you!

I know you are someone who wants the best for her life and who is ready to create it. You know deep down that your life is your own and that anything is possible. (Please note: if a little voice in your head just piped up and yelped, 'What? I don't know that at all!' – just ignore it for now, we will deal with her later!)

To get the most out of this book, there will be activities for you to complete along the way and I guarantee that your full involvement in doing these will see you rewarded. Be prepared to step up and take it on. This is your time! Time to stop being a spectator and get out onto the court - even during the times you don't feel like it.

When I work closely with people, helping them propel towards their goals, they usually start off very keen and inspired until that time when excuses begin to raise their ugly heads and get in the way of progress. I am sure I have heard every possible excuse for someone not doing the things that are important to them! It can be frustrating to watch someone with so much opportunity and breakthrough in front of them, start placing their own (usually imaginary) roadblocks in their way. Surprisingly, successful people have all the excuses come up for them too; they just see those excuses for what they are and give them a good royal kick out of the way.

Let's see if any of these ring a bell with you…

- I'm too busy.
- I'm too tired.
- It will never happen.
- My confidence is too low.
- It will take too much time and effort to change.
- I think I can get by with my current low levels of confidence.
- I never get what I want, that's just the way it is and nothing will ever change that.
- The kids come first.
- My work comes first.
- I'll get serious about working on my 'self' next year.
- My dreams are so unrealistic, so what's the point?
- This is just not for me; I'll simply read the book and tell everyone else how to improve *their* confidence.

Excuses are not unique to you. They exist in abundance for everyone. People who know what they want to create in their life have simply learnt how to find a way around them.

Unfortunately, I am not there to personally move you through these moments. So, you need to keep a very close eye on your excuses when they do surface and recognise their potential to put the brakes on you and your breakthroughs. Forget that spectator stuff; this is your opportunity to play the game - even when you don't want to. To win, all you have to do is stay on the court.

And, don't think that I can't relate. For instance, I am always too busy. That's my excuse for anything and everything. A friend challenged me on it once, asking me who managed my diary.

'Um…I do.' I said.

'And who agrees to take on the commitments that are scheduled in it?'

Your Moment of Truth

'Um…I do that too.'
'Well then, sort it out.'

She was right. I had to take responsibility for making myself so busy and stop whining about having no time. I wasn't the victim of some nasty 'time thief'; I was just wallowing in my own soft, squishy excuse and loving it. Everyone is busy! That is the way of the new world and, you know what? It's the way we like it. The 'I'm too busy' excuse has now become about as believable as the old 'dog ate my homework' one.

'Not managing your time and making excuses are two bad habits. Don't put them both together by claiming you 'don't have the time'.'

-Bo Bennett-

I challenge you to listen carefully to your 'reasons' for not giving 100% and see if they echo through various areas of your life. I have found that the excuses we use for not doing the little things are usually the same ones we use for not doing the really big things too. Remember, you are the only person keeping your excuses in existence. So, see them, hear them, pick them up and hold them. Then kick them out. You won't need them anymore!

If you get past these blockages, commit to the process of this book and use the techniques I will share with you, you will significantly increase your confidence and the way you feel about yourself and your life. You will experience a sense of choice you have not felt before. You will have a belief in yourself that will give you freedoms you have never encountered before. Freedom to be yourself, freedom from being stopped, freedom to be self-expressed and the freedom to create the life you want. It is worth every minute of the energy you will put in and the effort you will make.

And you, my friend, are going to love it. Ready? Let's do it.

The grass is always greener on the other side of the fence... until you learn to fertilise your own damn grass!

Finding Little Miss Confidence

One

From this point on, be prepared to put aside all of your comparisons about the state of your neighbours' grass. It's actually all about you and the changes that you need to make to get what you want. And know that you already have everything you need to make that happen.

What is Confidence? Blowing Open the Myths!

Confidence - 'The quality of being **certain** of your abilities or of **trusting** other people, plans or the future.'

–Cambridge International Dictionary-

Of all the personality traits, I believe confidence is one of the most sought after. We perceive that with confidence anything is possible. Self-belief is the spring-board from which we leap to achieve what we want in life and the driver that keeps us going. It is what gives us the nerve to take that risk, the courage to speak out at that meeting, to apply for that promotion, the spirit to follow that dream and the cheek to smile at that gorgeous man (or woman) on the other side of the room!

It is widely accepted that confident people are usually happier, more genuine and more content than those less confident. Generally, confidence lends itself to a real and authentic interest in others, a fun outlook on life and an ability to be fully self-expressed. Arrogance, of course, should never be mistaken for genuine confidence. They are poles apart and, in fact, the former is an unattractive mask to hide an enormous lack of the latter. The real thing is actually very generous and inspiring – and soon to be all yours.

We all have activities in our lives that we are confident about – that we *know* we can do. Think of something now. What do you have complete confidence doing? It could be a sport, a craft or maybe a skill within your career. Perhaps you are confident using a computer, drawing, sewing or even cooking a tasty spaghetti bolognaise. Imagine if you could feel that way about anything you wanted to do in life! What opportunities would be available to you? What would you attempt that you are not attempting now?

Let's look at the difference confidence brings.

Women with Low Confidence:

- Depend excessively on the approval of others in order to feel good about themselves,
- Avoid taking risks because of their fear of failure,
- Do not expect to be successful,
- Put themselves down constantly,
- Have an unruly negative chatterbox in their head,
- Discount or ignore compliments,
- Are less likely to effectively combat negativity and criticism,
- Feel more anxious and afraid,
- Avoid taking on new things in their life,
- Feel lethargic,
- Have higher stress levels,
- Are more likely to engage in unhealthy behaviour,
- Are more prone to enter into and tolerate abusive or unhappy relationships, and
- Have social difficulties.

Women with Good or High Levels of Confidence:

- Are happier and friendlier,
- Are more self-expressed and independent,
- Are more active,
- Have better mental and physical health,
- Deal with stress more effectively,
- Have self-trust and trust others,
- Have longer and happier relationships,
- Are more likely to carry projects to completion,
- Can more effectively deal with negativity and criticism,
- Are willing to risk the disapproval of others because they generally trust their own abilities and accept themselves, and
- Are more likely to engage in healthy behaviours.

So who do you want to be?

Despite our unending respect for confidence there are 3 common misconceptions that I need to deal with upfront.

Myth 1: People are born with confidence.

The first myth about confidence is that people are born with it, that it comes naturally, or that some are just lucky enough to have it. Not so! Confidence is a learnt behaviour and available to everyone. Possibly you didn't have confident role models around you so you never learnt from them the attitude or behaviours of being confident. And now, you have been low in confidence for so long that this has become a habit that is hardwired into your brain.

Maybe you were a confident woman once but your kids, life changes, career changes, divorce, breakup, weight gain, etc. gave you a right royal knock to the ground and it's been a long time since you've decided to get up.

Regardless of how long you have been living a life of low confidence, this is your cue to celebrate! By realising that confidence is a learnt behaviour – an attitude – you will see that your envying days are over, as you too will soon have that twinkle in your eye! Feeling confident within ourselves is a choice and that choice is about practising confidence techniques that give you access to a more confident way of being. If you continue these new behaviours and attitudes then a new habit of being confident will form and you are on your way again!

'... the most wonderful discovery about self-confidence is that it is a mental quality that can be learned with practice. Because it is so learnable, self-confidence can be developed and built up systematically and progressively over time...'

–Brian Tracy-

Your own Little Miss Confidence is kicking up her heels right now and singing at the top of her lungs, 'If you want me, come and get me!' With a clear focus, understanding of confidence-boosting techniques and the discipline to practise them, she will be can-canning her way over to you in no time.

Myth 2: Confidence levels are consistent.

The second myth about confidence is that it stays consistently at the same level or, once you've got it, you've got it for good. It's helpful for you to realise though, that our friend Little Miss Confidence can't be a carefree karaoke queen all of the time. There are going to be times when she drops the mic and bolts for the bathroom in embarrassment. That's guaranteed! Every single one of us suffers from phases of self-doubt now and then. Think of the woman you admire most for her 'can-do' attitude and know that her confidence dips regularly. She doubts herself often, it's just that she has become very good at throwing crafty one-liners at her annoying internal heckler.

Finding Little Miss Confidence

To avoid becoming disillusioned about your changeable confidence levels, imagine for a moment your confidence as a roller-coaster. It is a continual upward and downward ride. The problem is we think that the ride is controlled by someone or something else; that is just the way it is and all we can do is hang on for dear life and hope that we don't get thrown off altogether. Sorry, but that's not the way it works! The lows come naturally with the highs. So, when the downward slide begins, there is no need to panic because you are the one at the control centre. You can switch directions whenever you like. At any one time you can either build yourself up or tear yourself down…it's up to you.

For me, when a downward ride starts I immediately employ my proven confidence techniques to help change direction and pick up momentum again. I am not always great at employing the techniques quickly. Sometimes I just want to be down, feel sorry for myself and wallow in my own drama-filled existence. But hey, that's a choice I am making! Of course it's hard, but I know that as soon as I want to feel confident, positive and happy again I can.

Once that choice has been made, it then takes effort (sometimes a little, sometimes a lot). Just as we need a regular exercise routine to maintain high levels of health and wellbeing, we also need esteem-building exercises to maintain high levels of personal confidence. Being more confident is about learning, practising and adopting practical techniques that work for you and that you can use for the rest of your life. You see, the grass will always be greener over the other side until you stop wasting your time envying someone else's grass and start fertilising your own!

Myth 3: Some people never suffer from low confidence.

In a word – rubbish! Everyone has unconfident times in their life. That's guaranteed! Even the women who seem to be always confident, I promise you, they too have times full of self-doubt and low self-belief; times when their own Little Miss Confidence has packed up her bags and left the building. They doubt their ability, they feel scared and may criticise themselves. You may not see it, but it happens. The difference is that they manage these times successfully so the outside world never sees it. Whether they know it or not, they probably have something similar to the Confidence Program I am going to work on with you here to get themselves back out there.

With this in mind, I have some good news and some *great* news. The good news is that every human on earth suffers moments, days or weeks of low confidence. That's good news because you now realise you're not alone.

The *great* news is that if everyone suffers times of low confidence, yet they are still achieving what they want in their lives, then it is reasonable to conclude that moments of low confidence is not the problem with not achieving what you want. The low confidence times come and go for everyone; it's how you manage those moments that really count. I'm going to show you how.

Laying the Foundation

Building confidence is like building a house - you have to lay a very strong foundation. If that foundation is shaky the house will not be stable. Confidence is the foundation that we build our lives on. When we strive for goals or take on new challenges, we have to ensure that confidence and self-belief are there in concrete as our unshakeable foundations.

Similarly, if you want to build a skyscraper the foundation needs to be even more reinforced, stronger and bigger than before. As you gain momentum with your new attitude of confidence, you may want to take on bigger goals, bigger challenges and bigger life changes. When you do this, a strong foundation of confidence in your life is even more crucial, as is the need to work your confidence techniques more consistently.

Finding Little Miss Confidence

Start with this activity:

1. When do you feel most confident?

Go back to when I first asked you this question at the beginning of this chapter. What did you think of? Think of as many as you can and write them down. Write down anything that you are confident about doing – absolutely anything!

2. Now, imagine if you could feel that way about anything you wanted to do in your life!

Think carefully about the following questions and write your answers on the same sheet of paper.

- What would your life be like if you had more confidence?
- What would you attempt that you are not attempting now? Write at least 10 examples.

Keep this document close at hand so that you can refer to it at any stage and get in touch with the life you are committed to creating.

3. You need to see it!

Look over what you've written and take a minute to create a clear picture of the life you would have with increased confidence. Close your eyes and imagine how you would feel, what changes you would make and what goals you would shoot for. Splash around in this bubbly new world for a while and hold on to the feeling it evokes in you so you will recognise it later. This is your Little Miss Confidence.

PUMPED Points to Remember

Getting to know confidence:

- Real confidence helps you be happier, gives you guts, gives you better health and allows you to live the life *you* want.
- There is absolutely no reason why you cannot have oodles of it – you have as much right to it as anybody else does.
- People are not born with confidence and it doesn't come naturally. Confidence is a learnt behaviour.
- Just as we can choose to stay under-confident, we also can choose to develop it.
- Confidence levels are ever-changing – for *everybody*.
- We sit at the controls of our own confidence roller-coasters; it is up to us which direction it goes in.
- Confidence is the foundation we build our lives on so it's vital that we have a strong foundation.
- Having a clear and inspiring visualisation of a confidence-filled life will help you create it faster.

What you DO affects
the way you FEEL.
How you FEEL affects
the things you DO.
The things you DO affect what
you and others THINK of you;
which, in turn, affects how YOU
FEEL about YOURSELF.

Acceptance
The Key to an Unshakeable Foundation of Confidence!

Two

One of the major ingredients to being confident is acceptance, so this chapter is an important one.

If you get to the end of it and still operate at the same level of acceptance as you are now, chances are you won't increase your confidence; no matter how conscientious you are about everything else. Acceptance is the key that will open the confidence door for you. It's really that black and white, I'm afraid.

In this section, be prepared to take on the challenge and aim for a new perspective on yourself, on others, on your circumstances and your past. It's time to give up on resisting the way things are and learn to accept your life. Step out of the ring and shake off the gloves, the freedom you'll find will amaze you.

Accepting You

The Good, the Bad and the Ugly

Truly accepting yourself is, I believe, the most important thing you can master in your life. Now, I don't mean accepting yourself once you are a certain weight, or have achieved a certain level of success, when you look different, feel different, look more like her, own what they own, are smarter or prettier, when you have a devoted partner, when you're no longer renting or whatever else the critical voice in your head is currently telling you. I mean to love and accept yourself EXACTLY as you are right now. Accept YOU – the way you are…the way you were made…with all your faults, wiggly bits, personality traits, heritage, individuality – the good, the bad and the ugly! Yes, that means today!

Perhaps you are cringing and telling yourself that it isn't possible? I can almost hear you through the pages! The majority of us always have something on the agenda that needs to be done, fixed, changed, lifted, tightened, lost, enlarged or minimised. Unfortunately though, after we've changed the first item on our list, we enjoy only a short period of self-satisfaction until another desire for change promptly takes its place. I'm not saying that you can't lift it, tighten it, lose it, enlarge it or minimise it, I just encourage you to consider that these things are not going to bring you the life-long internal peace that comes with genuine acceptance and love of who you are.

The bottom line is that all of these desires for change plague us when we are mostly concerned with how we appear to others. If we could stop the constant comparisons to other people, we wouldn't have to live by anyone else's standards but our own. How refreshing! Now I know you've heard this before but now is the time to really take it on. Making yourself spectacular for everybody else is a losing battle, but pleasing yourself…now that's a different story.

I was extremely fortunate to learn techniques that helped me to achieve healthy acceptance of who I was from an early age. I am sure Mum did not realise what an amazing turning point it would be for me and my life by giving me Louise Hay's famous book, *'You Can Heal Your Life'* when I was only 15. It opened up a whole new realm of belief systems for me and it offered me a new way to look at my relationship with the world. It was profound and took me to a whole different level as far as my maturity was concerned.

Acceptance

I remember talking to girls at school about the book and about the new ideas and beliefs I was learning and they couldn't understand where I was coming from at all. They were reading trashy teenage romance novels and were not interested in my new-found personal development books. I began to shy away from magazines filled with diet tips, make up hints and guides to snagging a boyfriend and started to see the effect these were having on my friends. Where were the magazines or books teaching us to accept ourselves or teaching us that fear was a normal part of life when you were stepping outside your comfort zone? Where were the articles that summarised the steps when striving for our dreams and explaining that our bodies are not to blame for every bad thing that happened to us? Where was the information about loving yourself and your body, rejoicing in your strengths and cherishing your personality and uniqueness? Where I ask, where?

Even then I could see the awesome power of acceptance and the destructive nature of the fight against it. I was 15 and learning about my potential to create anything I believed in, to love and accept who I was and it was amazing stuff! It took loads of practice and a real focus on changing my thoughts, but the work always yielded great results.

One of the major techniques in Louise Hay's book is mirror work and affirmations. I was encouraged to talk to my reflection and say 'I love you, Jodie. I love and accept you exactly as you are.' The recommendation is to repeat internal affirmations constantly – all day, every day. So there I was, 15 years of age, trotting off to my Christmas holiday job silently saying, *'I love and approve of myself, I love and approve of myself, I love and approve of myself'*, over and over again. Crazy? Absolutely - particularly at an age when being told you 'love yourself' by your peers was an enormous insult! But the fact was, after a short while, I noticed an incredible difference. I began to feel free of the pressures I'd placed on myself previously – the standard teenage girl stuff of thinking I was fat, that the popular girls were better than me or worrying that because the boys didn't want to kiss me after school meant that I would never be attractive to the opposite sex.

Using this technique, I became no longer bogged down by what I thought others expected of me and that meant my breath came in and out a little easier. It was the first step to becoming happy with who I was and who I was not. And that's big stuff for a teenage girl. I came to understand that everything you say and everything you think determines the reality of your life and, therefore, all our thoughts and words are actually affirmations - either positive or negative. The reality is that we affirm absolutely everything that happens to us. 'Life sucks', 'It's all too hard', 'I'm going nowhere', 'I have no confidence'. Guess what? These are all affirmations! Not very life enriching, but affirmations nonetheless. So, every time you state that you don't want to do affirmations, consider this: You already are! The challenge here is to simply do them differently.

So yes, we are going to practise positive affirmations to change your thoughts. Has that voice in your head just started rambling on telling you this is all that mumbo jumbo stuff? Well, it's now time to listen and take note. This mumbo jumbo stuff works. ABSOLUTELY WORKS EVERY TIME. (Loud enough for you?)

To be honest, in the beginning I didn't actually believe they would work either, but I stuck with it and they did! Keep working with me here because I'll explain this in a way that you may have never heard before.

There are 2 MAJOR points you need to understand here:

1) Your thoughts create a field of reference; and
2) You will always prove yourself right.

So, we will start with the first one – Your thoughts create a field of reference.

Acceptance

Let's say that you decide it is time to buy a new car. This thought comes into your mind and contemplation begins. You consider the price you can afford and the make and colour of car you would like. You may start focusing on the idea of buying a red Mazda 3 as an example. Now, as you go about your life, you start seeing red Mazda 3s on the road as you drive to work. You see an article about them in the paper, you see a sale on one at your local dealer's and your work colleague mentions that she also has one. You are surprised by the number of red Mazda 3s around you just as you started having thoughts about buying one. You have created a field of reference for your brain for red Mazda 3s and, therefore, you notice every red Mazda 3 around you.

This scenario works with anything you start a thought process about or have a consistent thought about. I remember as soon as I fell pregnant with my first child I noticed there were hundreds of pregnant women around me everywhere I went. They were in coffee shops, on the train to work, at the supermarket, in restaurants and at the beach. I also started to see all the maternity clothing shops that were in my local area; shops I had walked and driven past for years without noticing.

Was all this an amazing coincidence? No. This is how our thoughts work. You see, the red Mazda 3 and the pregnant women were there all along. I didn't notice them before because they weren't in my field of reference. They were not something that resonated with me or my thoughts at the time. I may have noticed a pregnant woman before but it wasn't until I was pregnant myself that I started looking at her in a different way, with a field of reference. Now I was looking at how she looked, what she was wearing, how big she was and whether anyone stood up for her and gave her a seat on the train. Sure, I may have seen her before, but I didn't SEE her with any reference to me.

All your thoughts work the same – whether negative or positive. Let's say that you think you are unlucky. You have evidence from past experiences that say to you that you are unlucky; and you say to yourself and to others that you are an unlucky person. What is your field of reference in this example? That you are unlucky! Therefore, what you are going to see around you is all the examples of why you are unlucky. You will notice (just like noticing the red Mazda 3) that you missed the train this morning to work (unlucky), that you tripped over a bump in the pavement and spilt your coffee (unlucky), that you didn't win your kids' school raffle (unlucky), that you didn't get the parking spot (unlucky) and the list will go on.

Now, let's look at point 2 – You will always prove yourself right. It is a natural human trait to want to be right. We hate to be wrong so we try to do whatever we can to be right about our thoughts and opinions. There have been, and still are, wars over the need to be right – fighting over who has the right religion, who worships the right God, who has the right laws and who has the right way of life. We fundamentally want to be right and this affects the way we see the world around us.

Let's go back to the thought of being unlucky. If you think you are unlucky then you will find ways to prove yourself right about that thought. If you think you are unconfident, you will prove yourself right and, similarly, if you think you are a confident woman then you will find yourself to be right about that also.

It works like this:

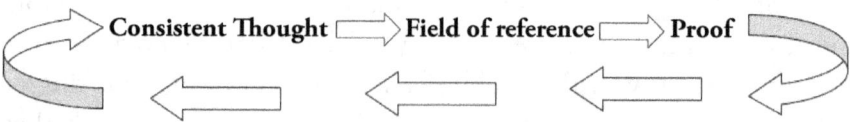

You have the thought, the thought becomes your field of reference and then you find evidence in your life to prove that your thought is right which, in turn, reinforces the thought and so the process starts again.

Acceptance

This process happens with all consistent thoughts that you have which is why it is absolutely vital that you monitor your thoughts at all times.

We all have the voice in our head that talks to us consistently but we MUST learn to control that voice, otherwise it will automatically run riot!

Think of it this way – there are 86,400 seconds in 24 hours. Let's say you sleep for 7 of these hours (less 25,200 seconds). This gives you 61,200 seconds when you are awake and having conscious thoughts every day. As you are capable of having a thought every 1 or 2 seconds, you could be having anywhere between 30,000 and 60,000 thoughts a day. If you don't make a concerted effort to think positively then how many of those thoughts do you really, truly think will turn out positively all by themselves?

Here are some examples that you may recognise.

Consistent Thought	Field of Reference	Proof
I am tired all the time.	You notice how tired you feel, how many times you yawn and how lethargic you are.	You are irritable and yell at the kids. You fall asleep at work and you're just too tired to get out of bed to exercise. The thought 'I am tired all the time' is repeated in your mind and the cycle continues.
I can't afford that.	You only notice all the things you don't have and can't afford.	You go to the nearest shopping centre and only ever notice the shops that sell items outside your means. The thought of 'I can't afford that' occurs again and the cycle continues.

My children are naughty.	You pick up on everything your kids are doing wrong.	You notice how well behaved other kids are at the park. This proves to you that your thought of 'My children are naughty' is the truth.
I am overweight.	When you look in the mirror you only see extra weight on your stomach and thighs.	You only notice people around you who thinner than you. You hate trying on clothes because nothing ever fits you like it does them.
I am always sick.	You notice every time you sneeze or cough and how unwell you feel.	You only notice when your kids come home from school with the sniffles and you assume that you'll always catch the cold from them.
I have no confidence.	You avoid social situations as they make you feel anxious. You only ever notice confident people in the world, doing what you wish you could do.	You only see all the people around you who you think are confident. You stop yourself from doing things because you don't believe you have the confidence to step up, volunteer, do the presentation, get on the dance-floor, etc.

What you absolutely need to understand in this process is that YOU choose the thought to begin with. The whole process starts with a thought.

Think of it this way – if you're not prepared to do affirmations and think positively, then what is the alternative? To think negatively

Acceptance

about yourself and the world around you? How do you think that having up to 60,000 negative thoughts a day is going to support you in your quest for your best life possible?

You choose every single thought that crosses through your mind. You have been thinking some of these negative thoughts for so long that you may feel that you don't choose them anymore, that they are automatic. But they aren't. You may have been told to think a certain negative way about yourself when you were very young. In fact, it's even embedded in our DNA to expect the worst. Thanks to our cave-man ancestors, our species is still essentially on the lookout for that sabre-tooth tiger or anything that may harm or threaten us. Our brain's only function is to keep us alive and, therefore, neuroscience studies show that we are constantly assessing the world around us for the negative and the dangerous. As a result, a positive thought actually needs a lot more reinforcement than a negative one before our brains can truly process and accept it.

However, it is not just simply our DNA that makes us think this way. You are also *choosing* to allow that thought to exist. The negative thoughts that you are having are there because you have created a habit of having that consistent thought. You have created a field of reference, you continuously find proof that the negative thought is correct and so you continue to have that negative thought. By continuing this cycle you strengthen the neural pathway of that thought. It's like you've built a super highway for it to travel along, quickly and easily. That is why it feels so automatic and that is why repetition of the new positive thought is so crucial. It needs to forge a new super highway also. (Let me tell you, this one is going in a much more desirable direction!)

The best way to change this cycle is to continually practise affirmations and to choose to think only positive thoughts.

Don't like the word 'affirmations'? How about 'optimistic declarations', 'constructive statements', 'positive confirmations', 'your personal mantra' or 'upbeat assertions'? It doesn't matter how you label it, the point is – just do it!

This technique of doing affirmations still proves extremely valuable to me and has been an incredible turning point for many of my clients. I am absolutely amazed when I talk to people and they have either never heard of affirmations or they have already decided that they won't work for them (even before the first affirmation comes out of their mouth!) Try them and see. Sure, you may feel really silly at first, but just keep going. You've got nothing to lose except that negative voice in your head.

Hints for Creating Affirmations

Always use positive words and phrase the statement as though it is already in existence. For example, if you say, 'I am becoming strong' or 'I will become confident' then your subconscious only hears that it will happen 'someday' and remember that someday, just like tomorrow, never comes! Turn this around to 'I am strong' and 'I am confident'. Use words that really work for you and create a statement that is easy to remember. Write it down and pin it up somewhere to remind you to say it until you get the hang of it.

Some powerful affirmations to try:

- I approve of myself and love who I am.
- I am fit, strong and healthy.
- Money flows easily to me.
- Everything is working out perfectly.
- I am safe. (A good one for comfort eaters!).
- I am totally adequate at all times.
- I am the power and authority in my life.
- I am free to be me.
- I trust the process of life.
- I forgive and release the past.

- I am surrounded by loving people.
- I am good enough.
- I deserve the best of what life has to offer.
- I express myself easily.
- I speak up for myself with ease.
- I am whole and complete.
- Intelligence, courage and self-worth are always present.
- Letting go is easy.
- I am confident, beautiful and deserving.

Let's look at acceptance of self in a little more detail. If it means authentic approval for the 'good' bits plus the 'bad' and 'ugly' bits, then we have to ask ourselves what (or who) determines what is good, bad or ugly?

Jenny's Story

Jenny was a client who kept telling me how awful she was because she didn't keep in regular enough contact with her mother overseas. When I challenged her on what was 'enough' she didn't really know. She just knew that it was something more than what she was already doing. As we investigated further she realised that at some point she had created a rule about how often she should write, phone or e-mail her mother. Then, when her life didn't allow her to follow the rule she had set, she made herself feel bad, wrong and guilty for it daily. We all do it; we all have 'I shoulds' in our lives that work against us, so maybe it's time to bend our own rules!

Recently I was standing with a group of mums when one of them was complaining about how tired she was, how busy her life was and how she just didn't feel she was coping with everything she had to do. She had 4 children, a husband who worked full time, she worked 3 days a week herself and she was also trying to look after her elderly mother who had been ill. I questioned her on the support structures she had for herself and she looked at me quite strangely. I asked her:

'Who does the cleaning at your house?'
'I do,' she said.
'Who does the ironing?' I asked.
'I do,' she said again.
'What about the cooking?'
'I do that too,' she said.

I said to her, 'No wonder you are tired, busy and not coping. You don't seem to have any basic support structures put in place for yourself.'

She looked at me quite puzzled and then said, 'But I'm the mum, that's the work mums are supposed to do. Isn't that my job?'

'It's not *my* job,' I said to her. 'It may be my agreed responsibility within my relationship to make sure the house is clean, that the clothes are ironed and dinner makes it to the table but I don't have to physically do it all. I have a cleaning lady that comes once a fortnight and an ironing lady that picks up once a week. I do the dinners on weeknights and my husband does all the cooking on the weekend. That is the only way I can run the house, run the kids, run a business and still maintain my sanity.'

'Wow,' she said. 'Do you really think it's ok to get someone else to clean my house?'

The exhausted mum beamed at me with visible relief on her face. In that moment, one of her 'rules' had been challenged. She had given herself permission to think a different way and throw out the old rule that she had to do it all. She could afford a cleaner but couldn't justify the cost because it went against one of her established rules. The revelation for her was not *which* rule could be changed, but the fact that the rules could be changed at all.

What rules have you set for yourself or that you think others have imposed on you? Remember, 'others' can be society, family, colleagues, friends, religious leaders, school mums, or authority figures.

Acceptance

Notice the 'shoulds' in your life and the areas in which you feel guilt, overwhelm and inadequacy. Also remember, there is a difference between rules and choices. It's ok to make deliberate choices in your life, what we're talking about here are the decisions you make because you feel you *have* to in order to follow an already perceived established rule. Now let's see if you can recognise which rules you think may be controlling you and try to turn the situation a satisfying 180 degrees.

Take a moment to write down any rules you can identify in your life. Here are some possible examples to help you get started:

- I have to be thinner.
- I must see my aunty every Sunday.
- I should always give reasonably expensive presents on birthdays.
- I must never show my frustrations to my mother…ever.
- I mustn't show him that spending so much time with other women bothers me (I don't want to be *that* kind of girlfriend).
- I must never cry in front of the children.
- I should be intimate with my husband 3 times a week.
- Good friends call once a week.
- I need a lot of money to be happy.
- I am … years old; I should be married by now.
- I am … years old; I should have children by now.
- A stay at home mum who isn't working shouldn't have an ironing lady.
- I can't start a home-based business until the kids are school age.
- I have to breastfeed for at least a year.
- I should exercise 5 times a week.
- I can't change jobs because I'm too old.
- I can't live with my partner before marriage.
- I have to go back to work once my youngest starts school.

- I must attend my place of worship every week to be good.
- I must restrict iPad exposure to 1 hour a week.
- I need to have …. (insert number) Facebook friends.
- I *need* to have a coffee to wake up on the morning.
- I *need* to have a drink to relax in the evening.

Investigate your rules thoroughly, distinguishing them from your choices and searching them for benefits to you. You may be immediately clear on identifying a rule that needs to change – that's great. It might take a while for you to explore exactly what impact your rules have on you and what you need to do about it.

It is also important in this section to realise that the people around you directly influence the rules you set for yourself. Sometimes the limits and rules you have put on yourself come from the people who influence you the most. Do you believe something because your mother/father/sister/best friend told you it was true? Are you stuck trying to apply old rules to your life that just don't fit anymore?

It's Just Who You Are!

The suppression of our natural personality traits is just plain dangerous. Resisting who we are and swallowing our instincts can actually make us sick. I agree with the belief that many of the modern afflictions that plague us today are a result of our inability to accept and express the emotions that come naturally to us. In the quest for others' approval, we have learnt to bury the feelings that are deemed 'inappropriate' rather than acknowledge, accept and take responsibility for them. It is time now to start the process of acceptance and stop making ourselves feel 'wrong' for being who we are.

For example, I am a very impatient person and I resisted accepting that for years. I tried desperately not to be impatient. And guess what? Denying that part of my personality only made it worse. I learnt that trying to suppress a natural part of who I am is futile. It

Acceptance

was only after many failed attempts at resistance and *trying* to be patient that I have come to accept this trait in myself rather than trying to hide or change it. I have accepted responsibility for my impatience and now understand how that quality impacts me and those around me. It's not good, bad or ugly – it's just who I am.

There is a perception in society that anger is a bad emotion and that people who display anger are bad and to be feared. It's not feeling the emotion of anger that is the problem, as anger often drives people to effect positive change in the world. The problem generally is the individual not being responsible for how they express their anger.

In this vain, there is a whole other extreme that scares me and I think is more damaging – people who suppress their anger (or any emotion for that matter)! The anger has to go somewhere. It doesn't dissolve just because they have denied it. It resurfaces eventually and re-emerges as things like violent anger, disease and depression.

Remember this is about acceptance of self. You are never going to get EVERYBODY'S approval all of the time. Be prepared to put a few noses out of joint. It's going to happen and it's perfectly okay.

You will never get full consensus from others that your actions, your decisions and your beliefs are right. Firstly, there is no 'right' – there are only different perceptions. What is right for me is not necessarily right for you or anyone else. Every human being has different values, contrasting beliefs and is on a wholly unique life journey.

As a woman, you need to choose what is the best or necessary option for you and your family and be satisfied with that choice - never waste energy questioning whether it was 'right' or not and never allow yourself to harbour guilt for those choices. Guilt will eat you from the inside out and cause you more damage than you know.

Sadly, we can be so affected by the opinions of others that we can become diminished as individuals and either too paralysed to take action, or end up doing what others think is best for us. Free yourself from the pressures of others' judgements and lead by example. We'll delve more into the acceptance of others shortly.

Being Special

On this planet, there have been billions upon billions of people alive before you. However, in the history of all mankind, there has never been anyone in the world like you - you are special. The past that has moulded you, the attitudes that drive you and the feelings that move you. Do you realise that nobody before or after you will ever come close to being anything like you?

You are unique, one of a kind. There is no one to compare you to. You are an individual with your own perfectly selected set of talents, skills and ideas that only you can offer. It is time to embrace your individuality. This is at the core of pure acceptance and an absolute necessity for achieving high levels of confidence.

Whenever I feel doubtful about something I want to do, I go back to this idea of being a totally unique human being. For example, when I started to write this book, the demons of doubt began cart-wheeling across my computer screen, trying to convince me that I couldn't do it. They tormented me with comments about how many other books there were and that I couldn't possibly compete with the hugely talented authors already out there.

To delete the demons, I worked at relating to myself again as the incredible, unique individual that I am. I started repeating the mantra 'there never has been and never will be a book that is anything like the book I will create.' With that, the need for comparison and competition fell away and what was left was just me as an individual and the confidence to get started.

Acceptance

A Tale of 2 Pots

'An elderly Chinese woman had 2 large pots, each hung on the ends of a pole, which she carried across her neck. One of the pots had a crack in it while the other pot was perfect and always delivered a full portion of water. At the end of the long walk from the stream to the house, the cracked pot arrived only half full.

For a full 2 years this went on daily, with the woman bringing home only one and a half pots of water. Of course, the perfect pot was proud of its accomplishments. But the poor cracked pot was ashamed of its own imperfection, and miserable that it could only do half of what it had been made to do. After 2 years of what it perceived to be bitter failure, it spoke to the woman one day by the stream. 'I am ashamed of myself, because this crack in my side causes water to leak out all the way back to your house.' The old woman smiled, 'Did you notice that there are flowers on your side of the path, but not on the other pot's side? That's because I have always known about your flaw, so I planted flower seeds on your side of the path, and every day while we walk back, you water them. For 2 years I have been able to pick these beautiful flowers to decorate the table. Without you being just the way you are, there would not be this beauty to grace the house.'

'Each of us has our own unique flaw. But it's the cracks and flaws we each have that make our lives together so very interesting and rewarding. You've just got to take each person for what they are and look for the good in them.'

-Unknown-

Finding Your Wings of Self-Expression

Recently, I was out on a morning walk when I saw 2 children of about 5 and 3 years of age, playing outside their home. What delighted me about this relatively normal scene was that both children were individually absorbed in what they were doing but each of them was singing loudly to themselves. Even as I drew closer and was obviously within ear shot of them, they didn't flinch – they just kept singing like it was the most natural thing on earth to do…and it was!

When we are little we can tap into our full self-expression and just let it cascade out of us. We sing, we dance, we speak our minds, we point, we ask questions, we laugh and we cry – all at the very moment the urge comes over us. Then, as we grow older, we learn that it is 'inappropriate' to do certain things as an adult. Someone makes us feel stupid for dancing to the radio in front of the mirror or singing passionately into our hairbrush, so we decide never to do it again. Boring! The rest of our lives are then spent resisting our full self-expression and suppressing it, even to a point where – given the chance to indulge ourselves again – we've forgotten what we would like to express!

With an increase in confidence, you will also start to experience a need to release your self-expression. This will come as your love and acceptance of yourself is strengthened and your need for others' approval reduces. Full self-expression is a wonderful sensation that will allow you to enjoy a level of fun, excitement and freedom that has no doubt been buried for some time.

My Funny Little Self-Expression Story

When I was a girl I dreamed of being a fairy. I wanted to shine in a flowing chiffon dress with sparkly wings attached; wear delicate ballet shoes, a halo on my head, glitter on my face and a wand in my hand.

I had always seemed to miss my chance to be a fairy (it was all about being Wonder Woman when I was young), so I was elated when I was cast as a member of the fairy chorus in my Grade 7 play. At the first rehearsal, quite unexpectedly, the chorus members were divided into 2 groups and my heart sank. As the petite little girls were

Acceptance

being ushered into the dancing fairy group I and the other taller, more 'big boned' girls were being placed in the second group. Then we were told that we were to form the second chorus group - the group of monsters!

In that moment I traded in my wings for a werewolf costume and my dream of being a fairy was shattered. As I grew older, the fairy craze really broke out among the population of little girls and mothers were dressing up their daughters to be beautiful fairies and they were everywhere. Every time I saw one of these delightful little creatures I had a rush of excitement and a terrible sense of regret that I was, and had always been far too big to be a fairy – or was I? As my confidence continued to grow and my ability to express myself fully expanded, I began to wonder…Hey! I would only be on earth once…didn't I deserve to indulge in one moment with wings?

At the invitation to be Mistress of Ceremonies at a company gala event, I saw my chance and decided to sparkle the evening up a bit during the awards ceremony. Instead of presenting awards in the boring old 'black dress' way, I arrived at the microphone as the official Awards Fairy. I was winged, haloed and wanded – much to the audience's delight! The evening's 150 guests were thoroughly entertained by the new spin on the boring awards ceremony and the event was a great success. However, nobody knew the enormous personal milestone my alter-ego represented to me – finally, I had found full self-expression in wings!

So, what is the biggest expression of yourself? It doesn't have to be something as outrageous as a public debut in your childhood dress-up dream, but I know there is something (if not many things) that you are suppressing. Whether it is your love of singing, your desire to dance or simply living moments in that spontaneous mode we all knew as children, there is something that shakes off the shackles and makes you feel exhilarated. It's time to find out what that is.

PUMPED

Start to look for opportunities for full self-expression. Don't worry about who might be watching, what people will think or that you may look silly. Who cares! Just be self-expressed. It is a freedom like no other and, not surprisingly, your release of self-expression will allow others to follow in your footsteps! People are always inspired by others who have the confidence to let go and be who they are.

Greater confidence will lead you to take steps to a greater level of self-expression. Maybe there has been a sexy outfit that you haven't worn for years, maybe you are desperate for a good old, fully expressed dance or maybe you want to sing in front of people like you used to? Or maybe it will be gaining (or regaining) the confidence to speak your mind and say what you think? Anything is possible with your renewed levels of confidence.

When my daughter was 2 ½ years old, I took her to Sydney's Circular Quay to see a kids' show at the Opera House. After the show, we were walking back to the train station when she saw a man, armed with a trumpet and a stereo, busking. As hundreds of people walked by this man on the busy walkway, she walked straight over and started dancing to the busker's music. She didn't worry about what people were going to think of her or what everybody else was doing, she just took action on what seemed a totally natural thing to do – if you hear music, you dance.

As she danced facing the busker, she had absolutely no idea and no care of the crowd that was gathering behind her. The bustling crowd had now stopped in their tracks to see this totally inspirational display. It was full self-expression on show and the crowd, who watched in an envious awe, couldn't wipe the smiles off their faces. It was one of the most beautiful things I have ever seen. Full self-expression is beautiful and very inspiring to those who witness its display.

So, what could you do? Ride the shopping trolley back to the car? Dance privately in your most daring underwear to the best songs

Acceptance

of all time? Make fairy bread for your friends? Sing loudly in the car (even at the traffic lights)? Wear those enormous earrings, that divine dress or those fish-net stockings? Dye your hair? Put confetti and sparkly stars inside a report to the boss? Start painting? Sunbake nude? Seriously! Just take a deep breath, reach down to your very centre and see what comes out!

Finding out what makes you feel brilliant, bold and brassy is no chore. It's the best time you will have had in a long time!

Eliminating Self-Hate Behaviours

All of our behaviours can be put into 2 distinct categories: Self-Love Behaviours or Self-Hate Behaviours.

The below examples will allow you to increase your levels of self-acceptance and confidence by getting you to start thinking about certain behaviours and identifying which of these categories they fit into. The key is to identify the significant self-hate behaviours and work on eliminating them from your life. Note: keep in mind that it is very easy to deny that we have any habits worthy of analysis, so be brutally honest with yourself here and the results will change the way you live your life…for the better!

Some examples of possible self-hate behaviours:

- Over-eating, binge-eating, eating unhealthy foods,
- Starvation or obsessive dieting,
- Not exercising,
- Over-exercising,
- Promiscuity,
- Drug use,
- Over indulgence of alcohol,
- Not looking after your emotional health and wellbeing,
- Constant self-criticism,

- Entertaining thoughts of self-doubt,
- Jealousy,
- Being a Workaholic,
- Carrying guilt,
- Harbouring anger,
- Continuous complaining,
- Gossiping,
- Being negative to yourself and others, and
- Creating drama in your life.

Some examples of possible self-love behaviours:

- Taking time out for yourself,
- Investing in a hobby or interest,
- Indulging in small luxuries like bubble-baths or manicures,
- Exercising whilst doing something you love (bush-walking, dancing, swimming),
- Meditating,
- Having healthy relationships,
- Eating healthy and nutritious food,
- Cooking or gardening for pleasure,
- Enjoying the company of your girlfriends,
- Delighting others with spontaneous moments of full self-expression,
- Giving a compliment,
- Self-acknowledgement, and
- Using positive language.

Now take a sheet of paper and divide the page into 2 columns: Self-Love and Self-Hate. Next, look carefully at your life and at all the different behaviours you exhibit. As you recognise each behaviour decide whether each is born out of self-love or self-hate and add it to the relevant column.

Acknowledging the behaviours you have listed in the self-hate section is an enormous step towards eliminating them from your life. Be consistently mindful of the destructive things you put yourself through and teach yourself not to do it by replacing the behaviours that are detrimental to your happiness with self-affirming habits. You will look fantastic, feel incredible and begin to see yourself in a whole new light. Revel in it.

Acceptance of your Past

Can you truly accept your past? All of it? Everything you've done, didn't do, said, didn't say and all those memories that continue to haunt you?

We know that there is no tangibility to the past and that all that remains of it are the thoughts we choose to entertain. Yet, our thoughts on times gone by and the feelings they evoke in us can drive us more than any other factor in our lives. By wrestling with the past, we are denying ourselves full access to what is real *now* and we are carrying the weight of things we cannot change with us everywhere. It's like carrying around the clothes you wore when you were 10 years old that you don't need or even fit into anymore. By choosing to accept the events of our past, we bring a newfound peace into our present and a sense of freedom to our future.

It has taken me years to fully accept everything in my past but it has been the most important process I have ever undertaken in my life and it is a continuing process. Piece by piece I worked through all the shame, guilt, resentment and anger that I had stored over the years, and worked on acceptance. I stopped hiding all those skeletons in the closet, dragged their sorry bones out and just let them be. I stopped blaming it on someone else, stopped trying to justify it, stopped spending countless unproductive hours wishing it were different – and just accepted it. All of it, just the way it was because really, it was just a bunch of old bones that were no real use to anyone. Oh, and remember that the past is 'just the way it was' according only to me!

Acceptance of your past is not to deny that terrible things may have happened or to try and trick yourself into thinking that the bad stuff wasn't as horrible as you remember. With genuine acceptance, your perception of your past may not alter, but your feelings about it and your attachment to it will. Consider the possibility of being at peace with all that you have been through in your life. What if your past was exactly the way it was meant to be? That you learnt from it everything you were meant to learn? Would you then be ready to put it to rest?

Your energy is far too precious to be wasted on guilt, resentment or regrets from the past. See if you can come up with any reasons that justify non-acceptance. Tough, isn't it? It is time to set you free. You are not gaining anything from the bitter taste of hindsight; quite the opposite, it's distracting you from living your best life now.

The way to be free from the past is to accept it exactly as it was, learn from it and move on. Everybody will have a different way of facing this challenge. I have met people who have a wonderful skill for simply accepting the past and others who find it a slow and painful process. Seek help whenever you need to, even if it means accepting support and guidance from a professional. No effort is too great in the pursuit of a happier and more productive life.

For me, it was about forgiveness; forgiveness of others, yes, but mainly forgiveness of myself. I sought help in books, tapes and workshops and really went after acceptance with determination. I didn't want to live half a life because of something that didn't exist anymore. Do you?

Acceptance of Others

Hush your inner judge

'Confidence and love go together. As you grow in confidence, so does your capacity for love. Greater confidence diminishes your need for approval. Paradoxically, the less you need someone's approval, the more you are able to love them.'

-Susan Jeffers-

Do you accept what other people do or think? Do you accept how they run their lives and their opinion on how you run yours? Are you judgemental, critical or defensive?

Until you accept yourself you will have a hard time trying to accept others. But acceptance of others is vital for your own confidence levels. When you are at peace with others, when you can accept their differences and demonstrate true compassion, you will release an enormous amount of negative energy, get on with living your best life and inspire others to do the same.

Hush your inner judge! Practise stopping yourself from making harsh judgements. Whether you are on the train, at a party, in the office, at the beach, with a mothers' group or out of town, if thoughts pop up that aim to pigeon-hole or judge somebody, stop yourself. Remind yourself that everybody, whether you understand them or not, is just trying to find happiness. When we really digest this fact, it becomes easier to see each human as a worthwhile soul moulded by the world. We can then acknowledge the choices they have made inside a life we will never know, and feel compassion for them.

Every human has a story of struggles and triumphs that you cannot comprehend by simply looking at them. When your stomach starts to clench with intolerance, tell yourself that you do not know what extraordinary life experiences have led that person to this point, and have compassion for their journey towards peace.

Whenever you feel the harsh eyes of someone else's judgement fall upon you, really take note of how it feels. File away that sense of injustice to draw upon when you next feel yourself sliding into judgement mode.

Avoid gossip and unfair discussions about other people. It is an incredibly difficult habit to break, but it reaps sensational rewards for absolutely everybody once you've mastered it.

Everyone is just trying to survive their own life. Be kind and compassionate. We are all simply looking for happiness.

No right or wrong - only perceptions

Just as we need to stop beating ourselves up for our so-called 'wrong doings', so too is the need to stop bashing others about the ears for the things we think they are doing 'wrong'. Accept that there are going to be times when you think somebody is doing the wrong thing. In the media, there is always a lot of talk about working mums; the 'fors', the 'againsts' and the 'in-betweens'. The interesting thing is that there is actually nothing to debate here. There is no 'right' on the subject and there is no 'wrong' on the subject; there are only different people with countless different attitudes, perceptions and experiences, each expecting one rule to apply to everybody. It is not going to happen! And, sadly, many mothers desperate to do the 'right' thing by their families are feeling the burden of a topic much bigger than their lives and circumstances, and suffering from guilt because of it.

Of course, this is not an isolated issue. There are many subjects on how others manage their lives causing veins to pop on foreheads all over the world. My point is that we could continue until the veins explode entirely and our heads fall off; we still won't make one way of living 'right' for everybody. In the meantime, the people we're so enthusiastically discussing carry on under the weight of our debate and try to manage the fact that there are so many people making them 'wrong'. This only diminishes the confidence of others around us.

The value of accepting others and their decisions is immeasurable!

Those damn rules again!

Just as you have placed rules on yourself, you will have also placed rules on others. What are the rules you have imposed on others that they may not even know about? Firstly, look at the expectations you have set for those around you and these will lead you to any rules you might have created. Next, we need to take full responsibility for setting these rules.

For example, you might have a rule about your partner saying 'I love you' at the end of every phone call because it makes you feel good and maintains a sense of intimacy between you both. If you have never communicated this expectation to your partner, what happens when they unknowingly break the rule? Do you feel hurt and unloved because you aren't prepared to bend this rule? And is this a shared value in your relationship? Does the act of them saying 'I love you' at that time mean the same thing to both of you?

I have worked with many clients on identifying the rules they have put on others. Once they are able to recognise the rules, they can then take responsibility for them. We usually feel disappointed, sad or angry when someone doesn't fulfil our expectations. However, we need to accept that *we* created those expectations; that *we* are responsible for the maintenance of the rules we set for others and that *we* are also responsible for our actions when they are broken.

Having the ability to accept others, even when they don't fulfil our expectations, is a challenging step on the path to gaining confidence. Keep on the lookout for proof of your own rules and be patient. Try always to see the situation from the other person's point of view and with time your acceptance of those around you will increase – along with your acceptance of yourself (trust me, the two go hand in hand).

Examples of rules we may place on others:

- My mother should call me at least once a week.
- My boss should say 'thank you' when I complete a task.
- My boyfriend should always offer to pay for dinner.
- My best friend should never say negative things about my partner.
- The bus driver should smile no matter what kind of day he is having.
- Our friendship group always buys each other a present for birthdays.
- My husband should know that him taking the garbage out is important to me.

Acceptance of Circumstances

'Resisting change is like holding your breath…if you succeed, you die.'

-Unknown-

Sometimes, life throws you a curve ball. You'll be moseying along, playing a great game of life and whammo! A curve ball takes you by surprise and completely throws you off your game. Now you can hate it, get angry at it, cry about it or throw a tantrum because of it, but none of these things will do you any good. However, the more quickly you accept that a curve ball has come your way, the faster you will see it for what it is. You can then respond to it and hit the bloody thing clear out of the park!

Acceptance

Alice's Story

When I first met Alice, she had recently been through a significant life change that had deeply affected her. Alice had been working for the same accountancy firm for 10 years before she was suddenly retrenched when the company went into financial difficulties. Security in her job and the regular income was instantly ripped out from under her when they handed her the retrenchment cheque. It was a curve ball that Alice never anticipated and it really made a significant dent in her levels of confidence.

What we worked on first was Alice's acceptance of the fact that all things must change, and then the belief in herself that she could handle anything that this new experience was going to throw at her. Alice's initial resistance to her current situation was negatively affecting her whole outlook and preventing her from moving forward.

You see, in the moment that Alice was handed the cheque, she only had 2 options: to believe that this was a terrible situation and resist the way things were, or to see it as an opportunity. Whichever approach she chose would significantly determine the outcome of what would happen from that moment onwards. (Remember how much of an impact your consistent thoughts can have). Unfortunately, Alice chose to let the demons of doubt take over her mind and she let the negative thoughts spiral her into the depths of uncertainty, anxiety and resignation. Not a great field of reference to work from!

Over the first few weeks, Alice and I worked on her acceptance of change, acceptance of her circumstances and her belief in herself. We had to stop the negative voice in her head before we could make any progress. Once she had this acceptance and belief, Alice was finally able to create a new field of reference - that this could be an amazing opportunity. From that point onwards, we were able to go about finding her a fantastic new job and move her into a more positive future.

PUMPED

This skill of accepting circumstances is a must-have for living a confident life. The confidence and belief that you have in yourself to deal with any situation that comes your way, will allow you to look the pitcher of any curve ball straight in the eye, wink and hit it square on. Expect the unexpected and be ready for anything – confident people always are!

Again, this is one of those skills that takes practise to really master. Heaven knows, I've been trying it for years and still the odd curve ball can send me into a state of panic, confusion and drama.

The best way that I have found to deal with the unexpected things that life throws me, is to stop…take a really deep breath…then repeat to myself…'everything happens for a reason…everything happens for a reason' and continue saying it (yes, even through the tears) until I start to feel that sense of calm acceptance that comes when you stop resisting the way life is. Sometimes it can take days but, I promise, you'll get there eventually!

I encourage you to find the way that works for you because this is such a key element to building and maintaining high levels of confidence. When you are truly moving with the natural flow of life and have stopped trying to swim upstream against the current, you will find an ease and grace to your life that will have you feeling free and unstoppable. Sounds good, doesn't it?

PUMPED Points to Remember

- Truly accepting yourself exactly as you are today is the most powerful thing you can do. You're ok, just as you are.
- Practise positive thinking consistently until you master it. It absolutely works every time for everybody and will significantly change your life.
- You are totally amazing and totally unique. It's time to realise how very special you are.
- Accepting the past will help you move forward. Your energy is far too important to be wasted on guilt, resentment and regrets from the past.
- Learn to accept others for the way they live their life. Everyone has an intricate past that shaped them into who they are, which none of us can ever understand. We're all just doing the best we can.
- The better you are at dealing with change, the better your life will be. Change in life is certain and confidence will allow you to know yourself as someone who can deal with anything that is thrown your way.
- Acceptance of the changes that happen in your life is the first step to moving forward successfully.

Truly accepting yourself exactly as you are today is the most powerful thing you can do. You're ok, just as you are.

Feel Fear?
Welcome to the Human Race
Three

'Self-esteem and self-love are the opposites of fear;
the more you like yourself, the less you fear anything.'

-Brian Tracy-

Is fear your friend or do you wrestle with it daily? Do you welcome fear, or does it stop you from doing and having what you really want?

If you look around, fear invades almost every part of our lives. We fear beginnings, we fear endings. We fear success, we fear failure. We fear change, we fear being stagnant. We fear the future, we fear the past. We fear taking on a new career challenge and yet in the same breath, we fear our future if we don't. We fear intimacy and commitment, but also fear being alone. We fear making decisions, not making decisions and making wrong decisions. We fear the risks of living fully whilst also harbouring a terrible fear of dying.

If you feel fear, you are not an inferior or strange person. The pitfall is to think that you are the only one dealing with it. No way! Fear is a natural part of the human experience and absolutely everyone is living with it.

Now, I am not referring to the type of fear that alerts us to danger – this fear is instinctive and necessary for our survival. I am talking about the fear that we allow to hold us back from our own personal growth, from living the lives we want and from doing new things.

We allow this fear to be destructive and it generates anxiety, regret, sadness, resentment, stress and a whole host of other negatives.

Being confident is not living with the absence of fear but about managing fear. I am always surprised by how many people truly believe that, as a confident woman, I don't feel any fear. When I am on stage presenting to a large group about fear, I tell them how fearful I was in the 15 minutes before I stepped onto the stage. How I stood in a bathroom cubical taking deep breaths and pulling myself together. There are always audible gasps of disbelief from audience members who can't fathom that the confident presenter before them was feeling fear only minutes earlier. The realisation for them about my reality of feeling fear is one of the main 'ah-ha' moments that audience members comment on the most.

This is why it is important to re-educate ourselves about dealing with fear. It is a matter of management, not a case of eliminating it altogether. It is always going to be a part of our lives; of that much we can be sure. It is a fact that every human being is feeling fear about a myriad of things, yet with so many people out there doing the things they want despite these fears, it is reasonable to conclude that fear is not the problem!

The issue is how we, as individuals, relate to our fears. It is only our own personal relationship with fear that leaves us either stopped dead in our tracks or recognising the fear and doing it anyway. For some people fear is accepted as a natural phenomenon and it, in turn, becomes a source of empowerment and excitement. For others, however, it is seen as a barrier or warning and it can be entirely debilitating, leaving these people feeling helpless and weak.

Consider that fear exists at the edge of our comfort zone. Every time you lift your gorgeous pedicured toes to take a step out of your comfort zone, they are going to twitch with hesitation. Whether it is to leap gracefully into an entirely different zone altogether, or if you are just considering a tiny step to the right, fear will be present.

Feel Fear? Welcome to the Human Race

What we are going to explore here is how to prevent you from placing those nervous toes back into your worn out slippers when there is a beautiful, stylish pair of new heels waiting to take you somewhere amazing!

To stay inside your comfort zone is to stay very much the same. There is no growth to be found while your feet are firmly inside your scruffy old slippers. Sure, they're super-comfortable and they do the job just fine, but you're not going to feel any new sensations when you slide your tootsies in there for the umpteenth time.

Everything outside of our comfort zone is frightening to a degree. The thing is, if we waited for the fear to go away before we attempted anything new, we would simply never move forward at all – let alone step closer to our dreams.

'A ship that never leaves the harbour is fundamentally safe but that's not what ships are for!'

-William G.T. Shedd-

It's time to leave the harbour and set sail!

We fear the unknown and, more often than not, we imagine it to be far more terrifying than it really is. The truth is that climbing into those new shoes puts us at a height we've never experienced before and our perspective shifts completely; a whole new world of ideas and possibilities presents itself.

Consistently pushing the boundaries of our comfort zone, either gently or with gusto, helps us move towards the life we want. **We actually get more comfortable with the sensation of being *uncomfortable*.** Daring to try something new and consistently doing things outside our comfort zone creates a reference point for experiencing this fear and moving through it anyway. And yes, this takes practise.

How to See Fear Differently

1. Re-educate Yourself

Acknowledge your current relationship with fear and create a fresh perception of it as your friend and not your foe. Remember, there is nothing wrong with you if you feel fear. It's a natural emotion - you may just need to change your relationship with it.

2. Have trust

If you knew you could handle anything that came your way, what would you possibly have to fear? That's right, nothing. It is important to develop a firm faith in your abilities to overcome hurdles. Life is unpredictable and there are bound to be obstacles along the way. When you place more trust in your capabilities, your fears will gradually diminish.

3. Get into action

'Half the things that people do not succeed in, are through the fear of making the attempt.'

-James Northcote-

Getting into action is the best way to deal with fear because action increases our self-confidence better than anything else. Every time you move through fear, your self-belief increases, as do the boundaries of your comfort zone, creating newer, larger and more exciting opportunities. You just need to take the first step.

When we 'just do it', the fear starts to dissolve because generally there is a realisation that what we had feared didn't happen anyway.

Feel Fear? Welcome to the Human Race

And each time you 'just do it', you're making future steps out of your comfort zone that much easier. Eventually, you begin to know yourself as someone who is not stopped by fear. How would that feel? Great, right?

My Action Story

For years as a single woman, friends encouraged me to try Internet dating. No way, I thought, there is no way on earth you are going to get me meeting men on the Internet! Looking back, it is clear that the only thing that stopped me from giving it a try was fear; fear of what people would think, fear of exposure, fear of looking desperate and fear of the concept as a whole – I knew nothing of this dark, mysterious world lurking in cyberspace. How did it work? What were the rules? How would I know who to meet with? It was all so unfamiliar and scary!

Finally, after years of resisting, I logged on and joined the virtual dating world. I was absolutely terrified. This was something so completely outside my comfort zone and nothing like anything I had ever done before. However, ultimately I knew that I could manage anything that came my way and I also knew that by giving in to the fear, I was only denying myself an experience that could possibly lead to wonderful things.

Over the next few months I learnt the ropes and was out and about meeting some fantastic people. I was having an absolute blast; my self-confidence was soaring with all this new-found attention and I felt exhilarated by the whole dating experience. I often wondered why I hadn't done it sooner, and then I'd remember: fear had stopped me, and yet nothing that I feared had come to fruition. Well, whether I was thought of as desperate or not I will never really know, but by this stage I was feeling so damn good, I couldn't have cared less!

I am happy to say that I did meet somebody very special through my Internet dating experiences and I ended up marrying him (cue the applause). By stepping outside my comfort zone and facing my fears head on, I met a wonderful man and we have created a wonderful life. Pretty good outcome really!

Often, one of the things that my clients are looking for in their lives is a relationship. When I ask them what steps they are currently taking to find that special person, they express that they're not doing much but quickly add that they don't want to try Internet dating. There's the fear!

Over the next few sessions we search for different ways that they can find a relationship and Internet dating seems to always end up on their list. I share my story, they start asking around and they begin to realise that this really is an acceptable way to find a mate in the 21st century. Ultimately, week-by-week we take small steps to push through the fear and finally they choose to log on-line and fill in their details. Once that step is done, they're away and generally, there is no stopping them.

I love sitting down with them weeks later to hear them talk about who they are e-chatting with and how many dates they have been on. You can almost visibly see the increase in their confidence. The fear is gone, their comfort zones have expanded and they are out living life and doing things they never dreamed they would have the courage to do. It is very rewarding for both them and me. They have begun to know themselves as someone who can feel the fear, move through it and get into action, and that resonates through all other areas of their life.

4. Become Comfortable with Fear

There is a famous quote by Eleanor Roosevelt that says;

'Do one thing every day that scares you.'

Feel Fear? Welcome to the Human Race

If you can do this, you will quickly notice the difference it will make to your confidence and your life.

What happens when you consistently face fears and step outside your comfort zone is that you become very familiar with the feeling of fear and, therefore, it doesn't knock you about so hard when it comes up. The first time I spoke to a room full of people it was terrifying, but I did it. The next time I spoke to a room full of people, I was slightly more familiar with the feelings that arose before a presentation so I was able to manage that fear better. The 20th time I spoke to a room full of people, I expected the same fear to raise its ugly head again (which it did) and I was ready for it. You see, it's not about eliminating fear; it's about becoming more comfortable with the feeling of fear.

Of course, feeling fear varies in degrees the bigger the step outside your comfort zone is, and that's why it is wise to take small steps outside your comfort zone as often as possible. I started with a presentation before 10 people and then gradually took on larger audiences. If my first presentation was to 500 people, then the fear would have been a lot more significant than working my way to that number.

In the end, however, *fear is fear* - so facing your fear of riding a horse will help you face your fear of speaking in public which will help you face your fear of applying for a promotion which will help you face your fear of publishing a book. It's all about just facing the fear.

This is why I ride rollercoasters! Rollercoasters force me to feel fear, which allows me to get intimately acquainted with that feeling again. If I recognise that I haven't been stepping outside my comfort zone for a while, or I'm hesitating to take on a new project because it scares me, I immerse myself back into that plastic covered seat and lock in the harness. The rollercoaster car then drags me back up to the top of its highest point and gives me the wakeup call I need.

PUMPED

My Fear Story - Learning to Fly

A few months after I had started my business I was given the opportunity, with a group of 15 or so other women, to do a workshop in trapeze. I imagined that we would get to climb up the ladder, have a bit of a swing around, have a giggle, fall into the net and it would all be over. Um…I was wrong.

We arrived at the venue, something they call a 'big rig', and it was e-*nor*-mous. I felt the nervous flutter of fear run through me the moment I saw it. Our instructor explained our first activity: we would each climb the flimsy rope ladder, step onto the skinny wooden platform, hook ourselves up to a safety harness, grab the bar, swing out, hook our legs over the bar, drop our hands (so we were hanging upside down), swing back, take hold of the bar again, release our legs and drop into the safety net.

I was gob-smacked! I looked around to see if I had accidentally entered the advanced course – they couldn't possibly expect all this from a group of women who had never done this before. There was absolutely no way I was going to swing upside down whilst zooming through the air at goodness knows how many metres off the ground!

We were then to climb up again, but this time we were to keep ourselves attached to the bar by our legs and execute a backward somersault to the net.

I was trying not to laugh! This was ridiculous.

The instructor continued (oh, puh-*leaze*). 'On your third and final 'fly' (circus speak) you will climb the ladder, but this time I will climb to the bar on the opposite side of the rig. On the count of 3 you will swing out, bring your legs around, hook them over the bar and let your hands go as you have already done. However, as you swing back the second time I will be swinging towards you and you are going to reach out, releasing your legs from the bar at the same time. I will be there, hopefully, to catch you. We will then swing once holding hands until we come back to the middle where I will let go and drop you into the net.'

Okay, now I was petrified. This woman was serious. Adding to my mortification was the knowledge, the absolute *certainty*, that there was no way I, or anybody else in our amateur group, was going to be able to accomplish the task put before us. We were beginners! What was she thinking?

Needless to say I was not the first volunteer to climb that rope ladder. However, what happened next had a huge impact on me. Our first brave group member climbed up, waited for the count of 3, and then swung out and carried out each of the instructions all the way to releasing her legs and dropping down into the safety net. She had done it!

I went from being ready to bet my life savings on the inevitable failure of a trapeze workshop to being in complete shock. Suddenly, my assumptions and firm beliefs were ripped apart by a woman who had courage enough to face her fear and believe in herself. Over the next few hours we would all take turns elbowing fear aside and believing in ourselves enough to fly! It was an experience we would never forget.

And guess what? Terrified as I was, I climbed that ladder 4 times and successfully completed the 3 flies that were initially requested. The last one with the 'reach out and I'll catch you' part took me another attempt but I could hardly believe it was me as I swung through the air, my legs hooked over the bar, blood rushing to my head, screams projecting from my wide open mouth, only to be caught on the other side by our trusty instructor! The adrenalin literally made me high!

What I gained was a lesson that I would never forget and one that I would draw on for years to come. This workshop forced me to ask myself the question, 'If you were so utterly convinced that you couldn't fly on a trapeze but, in fact you could, then what else are you absolutely sure you could never do, but actually can?'

PUMPED

I was lucky enough to get a glimpse of the limiting beliefs that I had unknowingly put in my own way and it was a great turning point, not only in the way I related to issues in my personal life, but also in the way I viewed my new business. There was simply no room for 'can't' - there were just unlimited possibilities. I only had to nod politely to the fear standing in my way and step around it to see what was on the other side; that was the only way I was ever going to know how extraordinary my life could be.

Just consider for a moment that everything you truly believe you can't do or have is, in fact, possible. What if your belief, no matter how true if feels or how long you have believed it, was completely off the mark? Are you completely underestimating what you are capable of?

Well, I would like to propose that this is exactly what is happening. What you believe are your limits, are **not** your limits. Fear forces us to underestimate ourselves and the only problem we have is that we listen to it.

Stop listening to it. **The one and only belief that you really need to have is that you do not know your limits**. Can you imagine what would be possible in your life then?

Isn't it time for you to FLY?

'You gain strength, courage and confidence by every
experience in which you really stop to look fear in the face.
You are able to say to yourself, 'I have lived through this horror.
I can take the next thing that comes along.' You must do the thing
you think you cannot do.'

-Eleanor Roosevelt-

Feel Fear? Welcome to the Human Race

PUMPED Points to Remember

- You are not alone, there is nobody alive that is immune to fear and knowing this should help ease any intimidation you might feel.
- The number one reason why somebody does not do something new: FEAR (don't be a statistic!).
- Spend some quality time with fear, get to know it a little better and get used to it being around.
- Fear can be managed; it's just a matter of knowing how.
- The more comfortable you get with the feeling of fear, the easier it is to face it time and time again.
- People can easily interpret fear as a warning not to pursue something, but an instinct to proceed with caution should never be confused with a reason not to try something at all.
- What you believe are your limits, are not your limits.

The more comfortable you get with the feeling of fear, the easier it is to face it time and time again.

Just Give it Up! Breaking the Chains that Bind You

Four

I have a saying that I use with my clients on a very regular basis that seems to really work for them. Whenever somebody is searching in vain for a sense of rhyme or reason about the way something is in their life, or they're clinging to something that holds them back, I simply say, 'Just give it up!' To 'give it up' is to not waste a morsel of another moment on 'it'. That's it. Finished. Done. Over with.

Here are the areas that most people tend to hang on to in their lives, and where 'giving up' is crucial to their growth and personal development.

- Blame
- The past
- Self-doubt
- Gossip
- Internal criticism
- External criticism
- Excuses,
- and, my all-time favourite…
- Guilt

So brace yourself. It's time to stop finding reasons, labouring over the details, searching for evidence, being right, being wrong or wallowing in self-pity. This is the only way to move forward from where you are and gain the confidence levels that you need to take on the world. Of course, it is still *your* choice. You don't have to give it up if you don't want to, but know this: clinging to 'it' will cripple your confidence and put a brake on your magic. So be prepared to drop every boring bundle you've got. Ready? Let's go.

Give up Blame of Yourself and Others!

Good news! It is now time to stop blaming yourself. Even if you are 100% percent sure that you are a dreadful person, and are totally at fault for the way things are, I am telling you to give it up. Right now, in this very moment, simply give – it – up. Don't debate over it, don't think about it some more, don't question why you are to blame; don't do anything except give up blaming yourself.

Not that easy? Well, in some ways it really is that easy! Stop allowing yourself the luxury of being in a place where you can beat yourself up regularly. That is all you are really doing. Nobody is benefiting from you being in this state of blame – not your family, not your partner, not your kids, not your friends and certainly not anyone else out there in the big wide world. Importantly, aside from everyone else, *you* won't actually benefit from the blame game either. So your best option really is to just give it up. Give it up now!

While you're giving up the blame you have on yourself, you would also benefit from giving up the blame you have aimed at other people too. Again, this is not serving you at all. In my experience, the person that you are making so wrong is usually oblivious to the blame-gun you have pointed right between their eyes. So, who is the blame game really hurting?

_____

Are you blaming others for the way your life is turning out?
That's like getting on a train going in the wrong direction and then blaming the train.

_____

-Unknown-

If you could pick up resentment, mould it into a compact missile and actually lob it at somebody, then you might feel a pang of release for a fraction of a second. That not being the case, you'll never find the satisfaction you're looking for. Ironically, the blame will eat *you* away. Just a tad counter-productive, don't you think?

What if you could stand on a table waving your blame-gun around, screaming out your convictions before pointing it into the face of the wrong-doer, *Pulp Fiction* style? Chances are your target won't care that your finger is on the trigger because he or she knows that your weapon is filled only with hot air. If they did care they have no doubt found a way of justifying their actions to themselves and to others, which has them feeling a whole lot better anyway! Perhaps, they are standing opposite you with an equally impressive gun ready for the Big Blame Face Off. Sorry, but you both need to get over it. You're not achieving anything constructive.

The only certainty about blame is that by clutching at the gun you are only exposing yourself to its pain, and lots of it. Put the gun down, walk away…and give it up. At that moment, you'll be free.

Julia's Story

When I first met Julia, she was angry. Really angry! She was angry about her life and had a massive blame-gun pointed straight at her ex-husband.

Julia had been divorced for over 2 years but she just hadn't managed to move forward. She had 2 kids, was resentful that she had to sell the family home, had not got back on her feet financially and was struggling to get back into the workforce.

As I tried to work with Julia to create a new plan for her life, she would revert to a barrage of abuse towards her ex-husband. Once again, I would spin the conversation back to her possible exciting future but it would only take minutes before Julia was spitting the venom of blame and resentment again.

Julia needed a wake-up call and so I put down my notes and gave it to her straight. 'How long are you going to continue to blame your ex-husband for your life?' I asked her, as I looked her straight in the eye.

Julia looked at me quite shocked at the directness of my question. It was obvious that nobody in her life had confronted her on her attitude towards her ex-husband before this.

'Um, but he caused this situation I'm in,' she started. 'He did all this to me and put me in this position and I hate him for it.'

'Ok but answer the question. How long are you going to continue to blame your life on him?' I continued, trying to not get caught in the 'who did what to whom' conversation. 'Give me a date. Will you continue to blame him for another 2 weeks, 2 years, 2 decades or will you just continue to blame him for the way your life turns out until the day you take your last breath and we put you in a box?'

Julia couldn't speak. She just sat there with a shocked look on her face as I maintained my direct eye contact, so she knew I still wanted an answer. Finally, the tension in her shoulders released and her gaze shifted down to her lap. After another minute, she looked back at me and there was a visible release of the anger from her face.

'I'm not sure I know how to stop blaming him,' she said in a soft voice, 'but I take your point; it's time, isn't it?'

'It's time,' I nodded. 'It's time for you, for your children and for your new life. It's time to start looking at the future and stop being consumed by the past. It's time for you to re-invent yourself, find yourself, to be the amazing woman you are and create yourself an amazing life. You can't do that while you are stuck blaming your ex for your life. So yes, it's time. Are you ready?'

She thought for a minute then, with a big breath in, said, 'Yes. I'm ready.'

After that very confronting session, Julia made fantastic progress. We worked on acceptance of her current circumstances and a vision for what she wanted her life to be. Then we formulated a plan to achieve that vision and Julia got into action, keeping her eye firmly on her new future.

Just Give it Up!

The first step, however, was to work on some confidence techniques and get Julia back into the game of believing in herself to secure that job she needed. Julia got a new haircut and colour, and bought a new outfit for job interviews. She looked great and felt a million bucks, and we never spoke of the ex-husband again.

Give up the Past!

'Should we all confess our sins to one another, we would all laugh at one another for our lack of originality.'

-Kahlil Gibran-

How much do you worry over things that happened in the past? How much energy do you give to worrying or thinking about what has happened?

Living only happens in this very moment. Nothing actually exists in the space before or after this instant. In this present moment, you have with you a bag full of memories that are yours and yours alone. These memories are your unique perception and exclusive interpretation of moments in time; nobody else will ever have an identical memory to your own because we each inject our individual opinions, feelings and attitudes into them.

If, as a result of your bag of memories, you live in your present with feelings of anxiety, resentment, sadness or anger, it is absolutely essential that you let go of your attachment to the memories that cause them. The past is over and unchangeable. Yes, it helps mould us - our values, our ambitions, our sensitivities — but it is not real for us *today*. Every moment you are offered is new, fresh and to be harnessed however you like. Please don't waste precious time living outside of the 'now' or, worse still, living in a nasty place in your past that you once knew.

Do not think that giving up your attachment to the past means condoning what happened. Obviously things can happen in our lives that cause incredible amounts of pain, anger and sadness; there is no denying that many of us will be forever changed by past events. The thing is we don't have to pretend that it doesn't matter, but by freeing ourselves of the pain, we are just not allowing it to hurt us anymore. You can't change it, you can't say or do something different and you can't erase it. It happened and now it is finished with, so stop letting the past hurt you. You have been through enough. It is time to give it up for good.

Oh, and if you are forever playing the 'What if?' game, you can now leave the court. Of course things would be different if you'd made a different move in the past, and you can spend as much time as you like dreaming up scenarios of how things *might* have worked out otherwise. However, I am here to tell you that the game of 'What if?' is impossible to win and is not the slightest bit fun – so give that up too. Later in this book we are going to work through the illusion of the wrong decision, which also significantly relates to the 'What if?' scenarios.

My Give It Up Story

I personally know all too well how difficult it can be to give up the past, so don't think for a minute that I am saying it is easy. It took me many, many years, counselling and personal development programs to work through my childhood relationship with my father. It wasn't until a personal 'ah-ha' moment of my own showed me how much the past was consuming me. I realised that holding onto this past resentment was preventing me from moving forward in my life and romantic relationships.

My 'ah-ha' moment was when I decided to make a form of peace with my father and called him after 15 years of being estranged. There was no course, no counselling and no one around. It was a decision that I made the moment I realised the damage that the past was doing to my life. I just made the choice to not give the past any more power and I gave up the resentment for good.

If you allow the past to consume you and fill your life, then there is no room for your present to occur or your future to develop.

Give up Listening to Self-doubt!

Doubt, like fear, is not going away. It will continue to nag at absolutely everybody until the end of time. So instead of trying to obliterate it we simply need to change the way we relate to it.

You are not the only one who thinks they can't do something. The thought just lives in your head. I doubted I could write this book until I put pen to paper. Then I doubted whether I could finish it and whether anyone would buy it so I guess if you are reading this line then the self-doubt I experienced along this book-writing journey had no truth. Why did I doubt my abilities? Well, usually we experience this self-doubt because it is outside our comfort zone.

We listen far too carefully to doubt and give it way too much power. As soon as the thoughts of self-doubt arise, we relate to them as reality or truth. It's not! Consider that doubt is just a question to an unknown. All it is saying is 'Are you sure you can do that?', or 'Are you sure this will work out?', or 'Do you think that is the choice you want to make?' It's just a question but instead of your immediate response being 'Oh, you're right, of course I can't do that', just take a moment to change your relationship to the question. Try answering in one of the following ways:

- 'I am not sure whether I can do it or not because I have never done it before – I'll give it a go and see.'
- 'I know I am making the right choice.'
- 'I know this is going to work.'
- 'I am a capable woman and know myself as someone who can achieve what she wants in life.'

Why do we naturally think that we can't do something when usually we haven't even tried? What would open up in our lives if we naturally related to ourselves as someone who can do anything?

When self-doubt rises and pushes its barrage of questions your way, thank 'Doubt' for its interest in you and then let it go. Doubt does not speak truth. Doubt does not speak reality. Doubt often does not even make sense. It's the answers to those questions that are important, so practise confronting Doubt head on so you can move forward to your success.

Give up Gossip!

'Great minds discuss ideas;
average minds discuss events;
small minds discuss people.'

-Eleanor Roosevelt-

Make the decision to stop gossiping about others and you will feel amazing. Gossip breeds negativity and a low, festering energy that you will not be free of as long as you indulge. Nothing positive has ever come out of gossip, so just give it up. It is more damaging than you know. Yes, you are going to be tempted into conversations with friends, family and colleagues about others, but when you are, simply stop and gently extract yourself from the situation. It is a very, very difficult habit to break but be strong – it's worth it!

It is true that our society thrives on gossip; so much so that multi-million dollar industries ride on the back of it. We love to read about celebrities and what they did and what plastic surgery they had…who they slept with…what terrible outfit they wore…that they have put on weight…that they now have a miracle diet (that you too can try)…that they're in rehab…their lives are falling apart and…and…and…! We pay for this stuff hoping that it makes us feel

Just Give it Up!

better about ourselves because we don't have the perfect body, we have wrinkles on our face, a few things are sagging and the Chanel designer outfit is not hanging in our wardrobes. And it does make us feel better, momentarily. We are relying on the degradation of somebody else to pep up our spirits about who we are! Not a very inspiring or positive way to feel better about ourselves, is it?

You know when you see one of those heart-warming, human spirit movies, where someone has beaten the odds and achieved the impossible or fulfilled their dream, and afterwards you feel uplifted, positive and inspired? Well, gossip magazines are exactly the opposite. They are so full of negative energy that it is oozing out of the pages and we suck it all into our life. THEN, we get together with our girlfriends and feed that negative energy and pass it on to them. Is that really what friends are for?

Can you imagine what a coffee with friends would be like if you all sat around and acknowledged each other, talked about inspiring stories, supported each other in achieving your dreams and were all full of positive energy? You would walk away completely alive and full of confidence! Now, isn't that what friends ARE for?

This was what meeting in a coffee shop was like with a good friend of mine, Raquel. Raquel and I met at a Women In Business mentoring program quite a few years ago, became friends and we would catch up every 6 months for a chat.

I always looked forward to these conversations over a peppermint tea as they filled me with positive energy and inspiration. Raquel is one of those people whose natural tendency is to see the glass half full and to believe in people more than they believe in themselves. She sees opportunity, capability and potential in everyone and this makes her a very special kind of woman. A simple one-hour catch up with Raquel would have me walking taller and believing in the direction I was going in my life. Whatever I told her I was doing, she would reinforce how amazing I was, how courageous I was and how much she believed in me – excellent value for the price of a cup of tea! These are the sorts of women who support you to be the best you can be and be the most confident expression of you.

Take the time to really note what feelings surround you when you participate in gossip. Imagine a life without gossip in it. Imagine the freedom and positive energy that would flow if gossip didn't exist. I cannot express how detrimental this habit really is – for absolutely everybody.

So why not replace 'Did you hear?' conversations with positive conversations that benefit those around you. Support one another, care for one another and inspire each other.

Go on, you know you want to.

Give up Internal Criticism!

Listen for a moment and you may soon hear the voice of criticism inside you. It is criticising your body, your behaviour, your parenting skills, what you cook, what you eat, how the presentation went at work and your competence in almost everything.

When are we going to learn that criticism doesn't work? Now, that's when! We would avoid a friend or family member who constantly criticised us, yet we entertain these internal criticisms day in and day out. Imagine how you would feel if you put an end to ALL self-criticism. Yes, absolutely all of it. I don't care if you hate the look of your thighs. I am not bothered in the slightest if you think you are too tall, too short, too fat, too thin, too loud, too quiet or too critical! Enough is enough.

I guarantee that if you gag your internal critic for a whole day, you will feel utterly wonderful. If you grab your critic's loudspeaker, shove it down her gob and leave it there for an entire week, you'll find yourself producing great things. If you demolish your internal critic's viewing box and make sure she's out cold for a whole year, you will, without a doubt, have the best year of your life. Get your heels on, step up! It's time for that internal critic to go!

Just Give it Up!

Actually, your best weapon against your own criticisms is self-acknowledgement and positive affirmation. Regularly dousing yourself with positive reinforcement is one of the most powerful habits you can form in your life and, when used liberally, it will keep your internal critic under control. There is a very powerful technique later in this book called the Daily Acknowledgement Diary, which will sort out this internal critic for good!

Give up External Criticism!

Of yourself

Just as we give our internal voice of doubt too much power, we usually underestimate the power of our external voice. Understanding how much of an impact our words have on ourselves and on others is crucial to building our confidence levels.

Firstly, I am going to ask you to give up the verbal criticisms of yourself; all the things you say to express how average you are. Stop it! It is not serving you at all. Even if you are 'only joking', please give it up. Our subconscious mind does not have a sense of humour. Whatever you say is what your sub-conscience hears and what it creates – so be careful what you say to get a giggle.

When I was single and in my 30s, I would meet people who would ask if I was married or had any children. I would jokingly reply, 'Oh heavens no, I can't even get a date!' One day it occurred to me that I was creating my reality with these wisecracks. Consistently putting the message out there that I couldn't get a date meant that (you guessed it) I couldn't get a date! However, when I woke up to these expressions of external criticism, when I stopped making these comments and stopped criticising myself about being single to others - yep, hallelujah, I got me some dates!

Keep a very close eye on what messages you are putting out into the world about yourself (seriously or otherwise), and give up the negative ones. Perhaps you can already identify an area (or two!) in your life where your progress is being affected by your words. Well, now you know...be vigilant and come out smiling.

Of others

I am going to express the importance of giving up your external criticisms of other people. This goes hand in hand with giving up on gossip. External criticism of others is obviously damaging to the person it is aimed at but, did you realise, it is actually just as harmful to you?

By criticising someone (or some*thing* for that matter), you are taking an internal negative and giving it power by keeping it in existence and expressing it externally. More than that, you are giving it permanence by sharing it with the world. You not only surround yourself with negative energy but you also pass it on to whomever you are expressing your criticisms to. Only an extremely skilled person will be able to prevent taking on your negative energy so consider that you are actually poisoning the environment around you. Have you ever been around someone who is criticising, complaining or whinging about everything? Even spending a short time with them will sap you of your energy. You will be trying to fight off the negative onslaught they are exuding and, if you are anything like me, you will become increasingly frustrated and angry. Not a desirable state at all.

Socially expressed negatives are like flu germs - if you put them out into the atmosphere, they spread to others and keep the virus alive. Shielding our mouths when we cough is what we have to do mentally with our criticisms. Put your hand there - just don't say it, write it or post it!

Naturally, you may continue to have critical thoughts of others. It is a significant challenge to eradicate these thoughts completely and we know that suppressing negativity is dangerous. The trick is finding a way to express these thoughts without actually giving them to somebody else. How? Try this:

Just Give it Up!

The Mind Dump

Find yourself some quiet time, and just start writing. Don't edit, don't worry about spelling or grammar – just write. Dump all your thoughts onto paper no matter what they are, and keep writing until you are completely out of words and the emotion is exhausted. Express everything you want to say, no matter how irrational it may seem. Then, when you are finished, destroy the pages. Burn it or rip it into a million pieces. Destroying this is vital – you need to be responsible for your output and never allow it to be misinterpreted by someone who may find it. This final step will give you closure.

Give up Excuses!

There's not enough time...it's too cold...it's too hot....but it's the end of summer...but it's the start of winter...I'm just too busy...It's that time of the month...it's half way through that time of the month... it's the start of the week...it's the end of the week...It's too hard...but my kids need me...but my work needs me...oh but I'm interstate...but I haven't done it in years...etc

---

'Get out of your own way;
most of your excuses for underachievement
are figments of your imagination.'

-Brian Tracy-

It's the excuses that keep you gridlocked! Excuses are easy to come by and easy to think of. When I wake up knowing I have committed to going for a morning walk, I can instantly think of a number of really good excuses not to do it. They appear from nowhere and start fighting with my mind trying anything and everything to keep me under the blankets. I sometimes have to work so very hard to ignore them; to see them for what they really are: a barrier between myself and my goals. Sometimes I win and sometimes…I don't. When the excuses hit all the right spots and have me at their mercy I stay put. Then inevitably, I kick myself later and vow to be stronger next time.

We have an amazing ability to create fresh and fabulous excuses all the time. I can come up with 20 excellent excuses not to eat healthily this week before you could say 'Fancy a hunk of mud cake?' Unfortunately, there are no prizes on the excuse game wheel. I don't get awarded points for the number of excuses I can come up with and I don't even win a prize. All I end up with is a bunch of elaborate excuses that prevent me from achieving my real desires. Not a very fun game if you ask me!

Remember that even the brain of a highly confident woman throws excuses at her constantly. It is what she does with those excuses that make the difference. There is skill and power in not being stopped by them. Don't buy into the conspiracy of them trying to stop you from having what you want. Practise ignoring them and it will become easier (just don't ask me if I would like some of that mud cake on a day when my weakness is low!)

So, give up the excuses. Just give them up! See them for what they really are - excuses. Not right, not truth, not really how it is - just a whole bunch of excuses that anyone could find and really, there is no skill in that.

Give up the Guilt!

'There's no point in being crippled by guilt.
Simply acknowledge to yourself that you have done something wrong, learn by it, and get on with the rest of your life.'

-Anonymous-

Allowing guilt to take hold of you is like inviting a monster to climb down your throat and infect you from the inside out.

Just Give it Up!

If you are torturing yourself over something, you need to understand that it is producing nothing positive for you or for anybody else involved. If we think that shutting ourselves down or denying ourselves joy is a display of remorse for what we have done, we need to realise that it is having no impact on the situation other than to make it more heart-wrenching. Surprisingly though, I find that clients can harbour guilt over an action taken half a life-time ago, or over thoughts nobody else knows about - even a comment made to someone who has since passed away. This is utterly destructive.

Guilt hangs heavy from your heart and it pulls everything inside you down. Carrying that weight with you in life is exhausting and completely inhibiting. If you can identify with that feeling, you need to ask yourself what it is for. How is guilt changing the situation? You are alive. You are a special, wonderful, incredible woman. Perhaps you could have done something differently and perhaps you couldn't have. It doesn't matter now. Feeling guilty will not change the outcome. All you can do is recognise and accept what happened, learn the lesson (if there is one), and then move on.

Guilt can stem from thoughts of what you have done, what you haven't done or what you believe you should have done. It can also raise its ugly head when you are faced with external opinions, or what other people believe you should or should not be doing. Whether these opinions come from the media, your friends, or just society in general, they can often lead to feelings of guilt and inadequacy.

Enter our old friend mother-guilt – 'I should have breastfed for longer', 'I should *not* have gone back to work', 'I *should* have gone back to work', 'I should spend more time with my family', 'I should have enrolled my child in the best high school… *before* they started kindergarten', 'my kids spend too much time on the iPad/watching TV/playing X-box…' and a myriad of other guilt trips that exist for today's mothers!

PUMPED

And guilt doesn't always have to be just about the big stuff either. If you associate guilt with the small pleasures in life, you are choosing grief over joy. If you regularly deny yourself wonderful things because of the dread you feel over it, you are your own worst enemy. Think for a moment about all the things you make yourself guilty for and prepare to see them in a whole new light (and let's face it, that can only be a good thing!).

Perhaps you can relate to feeling guilt about some of these?

I should not have:

- Had that piece of cake,
- Skipped the gym,
- Had time to myself this afternoon to recharge,
- Forgotten to call my brother for his birthday,
- Left the washing out in the rain again.

Don't *think* about giving it up; don't consider giving it up tomorrow; give it up right this moment. That's right, all of it. Sever the connection to guilt and feel yourself grow lighter, stronger and happier. Understand that you are not letting anybody down by not feeling the guilt anymore. You did the best you knew how at the time and now that time is over.

Whatever it is, just give it up! It's time to get on with the rest of your life!

Accept it or change it.
Don't feel guilt over it.

Just Give it Up!

PUMPED Points to Remember

- It's time to STOP the blame game for yourself and everybody else. It is what it is. It was what it was. Nobody is benefitting from the blame game, so it's absolutely time to set yourself free.
- I get it – the past was hurtful, painful and/or disappointing – but hanging onto it only brings that hurt, pain and disappointment into the now. Wasn't it bad enough the first time? Why keep re-living it? Do what you need to do to let it go!
- We all have self-doubt and yet others are getting on with life so the presence of self-doubt is not the problem. The problem is how we relate to that doubt when it arises.
- STOP gossiping! Have positive, inspiring, motivating conversations and watch your life take off.
- STOP the criticism. It's absolutely holding you back. Turn it around now to start the best year of your life.
- There's NO prize for coming up with the best excuse. You're just cheating yourself. Make your life a 'No Excuses Zone' to dramatically increase your chances of getting the life you want.
- The guilt eats you alive! You want wellness and a great life? Then give up the guilt from your past, from your choices, from your situation or any other guilt you hold. Accept it or change it – that's it!

Doubt does not talk truth. Doubt does not talk reality. Doubt often does not even make sense.

Responsibility

Five

Seeing Responsibility Differently

Taking 100% responsibility for your life can be one of the hardest belief systems to implement. I was first introduced to this concept whilst reading the book my mother gave to me – '*You Can Heal Your Life*' by Louise Hay. I have been trying to master it for years and still, I find myself wavering, trying to find someone or something to blame or to be responsible for the way things turned out in my life.

If you don't take full responsibility genuine confidence will tend to elude you. However, 100% responsibility is one of the most challenging 'life renovations' to implement. So be patient with your progress and expect to be working on it indefinitely. The concept of full responsibility can also be tricky to understand when it is new to you, so let me first explain exactly what we will be exploring here.

The formula for responsibility is quite self-explanatory:

Responsibility = Response + Ability = our ability to respond to a situation.

Responsibility, in this context, is also directly related to power. If you take full responsibility for a situation then you are taking power over your ability to respond to it. This allows you to take control and move to change it. Denying full responsibility is to remain at the mercy of the problem and as a victim of its negative effects.

I hear clients say, 'but if I take full responsibility, that will mean I am completely to blame for everything.' Not so. It is not about blame or who was wrong. Don't get caught in the trap of taking full responsibility just to make yourself wrong, or accept all the blame. It's about being able to take full responsibility because this is the ONLY way you can regain your power.

For instance, imagine you are working with somebody that you find absolutely impossible to deal with (not so difficult to imagine?). You find yourself exacerbating over the relationship with your colleagues and harping on about it to your partner whose eyes glaze over at the very hint of the subject.

This is not just a temporary upset. This is something that is affecting your happiness at work and having a considerable impact on your wellbeing, not to mention probably boring the life out of some poor committed souls around you. This difficult relationship is beginning to consume you and there is no obvious light at the end of the tunnel.

If you were to take 100% responsibility for this situation, you would stop blaming your colleague for your frustrations. You would accept the situation for what it is and acknowledge that you alone own the negativity you feel as a consequence of it. The question would then be, 'How do I transform this problem into something positive for myself and for others?' You might choose to harness your sense of dissatisfaction and make that bold career change you have been considering. You may opt to confront the person involved and discuss your issues with the aim of revolutionising your working relationship. You may choose to minimise the amount of time you are working with this person so you can reduce your frustration levels. There are numerous possible solutions. The point here is that *you* are taking full responsibility and, therefore, complete control of how the situation progresses.

In contrast, refusing responsibility would mean agreeing to continue to be consumed by your own frustration indefinitely. In the wait for your colleague to get a personality transplant and magically steal all of your negativity from you, you would carry on complaining to other members of staff, you would ignore your partner's sighs

Responsibility

and persist with blow-by-blow character breakdowns, and you would grow more angry, demotivated and bitter by the day.

In this instance you would be working inside the 50% responsibility rule which is: when they sort out their 50% of this problem, then I'll sort out mine! Or perhaps you'd create a 0% rule to stick to: this person is completely and utterly to blame for my unhappiness and nothing is going to improve until they do! I hate to tell you this, but it's not going to happen. It is all or nothing and the ball is well and truly in your court.

If you are beginning to notice a pattern emerging from the lessons in this book, you're spot-on: it is *your* choice. Whether you aim incessant blame at your colleague and accept no responsibility for your responses, or accept the challenge and administer change, is completely up to you. Take it on! You have everything you need to remedy the situation you're feeling terrible about and frankly, it is your responsibility and nobody else's – so make your choice.

'Between stimulus and response, there is a space. In that space is our power to choose our response. In our response lies our growth and our freedom.'

-Unknown-

Mary's Story

A client of mine, Mary, was working on her goal of weight loss and improved body image. She had tried many diets over the years and was completely disheartened by the fact that, although they would work initially, the weight would inevitably return and the cycle of frustration would continue.

Together we discovered that in the early stages of each weight loss program that Mary employed she felt full responsibility for her body and was choosing to take action. And it worked. However, once the weight was coming off, Mary's sense of responsibility would waver and the old excuses and habits would creep back. In this situation, full responsibility equals positive results. When 100% responsibility is not taken, Mary loses control of her weight and feels like the victim of a rogue, delinquent body.

In the early stages of our coaching I shared my own personal weight loss journey with Mary. Her passing comment that I was 'lucky' with my body shape was quickly corrected when I explained to her that luck had nothing to do with it. It was about my ongoing choices. There was a turning point in my life where I committed to a healthy eating program, lost 15 kilos and became a lifetime member of Weight Watchers. I had taken back the power over my body by accepting *full responsibility* and making the necessary choices to achieve my desired outcome, and I knew this was for life.

Over the next few weeks I worked with Mary on taking and maintaining full responsibility for her weight. If she was busy and didn't make time to do her exercise, then *she* was completely responsible for that. If she was in a restaurant for lunch that didn't offer healthy options only *she* was responsible. If she ate the cake, only *she* was responsible for lifting that cake fork and putting it in her mouth.

Mary also started to realise and accept that she would consistently be watching her weight for the rest of her life. It was unlikely that her metabolism was going to morph into one that would allow her to eat her body weight in cream buns and not gain a kilo. Mary had to take full responsibility for maintaining a healthy weight for life, which meant managing her eating and exercise for life also.

Mary finally accepted the power of her ability to respond to her body and, in the years since her coaching series, has simply done what she needs to do to keep her weight the way she wants it. The responsibility stays put and the weight stays off - just like that.

Responsibility

Mum's Story

The most inspiring person I have ever known was also someone who taught me just how interconnected responsibility and power actually are.

In her mid-30s, with 3 children and a marriage breaking down, Mum was told she had a brain tumour that was growing behind her left eye. Doctors did not know how long she would have to live or whether surgery to remove the tumour was even an option. Obviously, Mum was devastated and she spent many weeks questioning why this had happened to her; what had she done to deserve such a thing and what would happen to the care of her 3 children? She could not fully process the reality of her situation and battled daily with her prognosis.

However, as the initial shock dissolved, Mum decided to make another choice. She chose to take full responsibility for the tumour and to do whatever was required to heal herself as best she could. She stopped resisting it and accepted that a brain tumour was now a part of her life and that she would need to live differently if she was going to get the most out of the time she had left.

Mum read books, researched her condition thoroughly and modified her life appropriately. She began to believe, that by living with the destructive amounts of stress from the failing marriage and clinging to deep resentments from her past, she was giving the tumour full permission to ravage her body. Mum worked tirelessly on ways to release the pressure and anger she was feeling and began to notice an enormous difference in her emotional and physical wellbeing. She was, of course, now playing with her life.

After a few years of great efforts to change her life, Mum's tumour had stopped growing and was no longer an immediate threat to her life. We believe this was completely attributed to the incredible turnaround in Mum's lifestyle, attitude and acceptance. By taking 100%

responsibility for allowing the brain tumour to exist, Mum gave herself the power to take action to cure herself. You see, if she accepted that she created it, then logically she could control it and stop it! This is a remarkable story and one that dramatically changed our family's life. I hope you can see the difference a sense of power makes in a situation like this versus the perception of a victim.

Taking full responsibility gives you the opportunity to affect the way things are rather than feeling trapped and powerless. Being responsible gives you choices and puts you in the driver's seat. Pedal to the metal, girlfriend!

Circumstances often present us with opportunities to change our lives. It is how we choose to respond to the circumstance that will always have the most direct effect on the outcome.

The first step to taking responsibility for your life is to realise that you have power in every given situation; you just sometimes choose to give it away. Nobody can snatch your power from you or bully you into remaining without it. Sometimes you may feel that you have relinquished your power because you just don't have the strength to fight for it anymore, or you believe that people and/or circumstances in your life have forcibly taken that power from you.

I get it! It is easier to feel like the victim of other people's choices and the power you think they have over you. It's rife in our society - we blame our parents, the government, our partner, insurance companies, our children, the driver behind us, the weather – anyone and everyone. When you reach the point, however, where you can take full responsibility for granting power to others and/or circumstances, then you can attempt to take it back again.

Ask yourself the following questions:

- What areas in my life do I feel I have no power?
- Who have I given my power to?

Responsibility

- How can I change the way that I am responding to this situation?
- What opportunities can arise from this circumstance depending on my ability to respond to it?

What you focus on inevitably expands. By overthinking a situation and only focusing on the problem and all the negativity associated with it, you are giving that problem increasingly more substance, form and power over you. You literally strengthen the neural pathways relating to that situation. Instead, try redirecting your focus on changing your response to the circumstance, and concentrating more on the solution rather than the problem. Focusing on the solution is where you want your power to lie.

OK, so let's have a look at a few areas in our lives where taking responsibility will always result in positive outcomes.

Responsibility for your Commitments

Are you being responsible for what you commit to? Are you able to say 'No'? Are you always busy and blaming everyone else?

This is one of the areas I struggle with. Sometimes I find it challenging to take responsibility for my busy life until I remind myself that I am the one making the choices about what I commit to. If I am complaining about something that I have committed to, but really don't want to do, then it is only me who isn't taking responsibility for that commitment.

Integrity is born out of the instinct to do exactly what you say you are going to do. If you notice that you slip and slide around certain commitments you have made, you need to take full responsibility for them immediately. Stressing, whinging and resisting the commitment will inevitably create a negative outcome.

Feeling as though you must always say yes to others, despite your yearnings not to, is a perfect example of placing your power squarely in the hands of somebody else. Take 100% responsibility for your will, your freedom and your desires, and choose to honour them. There is no power in blaming someone else if they asked you to do something and you said 'Yes', because you weren't strong enough to say 'No'. You are responsible for your commitments. Be assertive, practise saying 'No' and commit to creating the schedule you want to have.

Responsibility for your Negative Chatterbox

There is a nasty old lady sitting on a rocking chair, peering through the dusty lace curtains in your mind. Her once soft, open face has been twisted by the sour words she speaks, and her thoughts on your world are not in the least bit uplifting. She thrives on the downside and has the ability to sniff out the merest hint of a negative viewpoint that might be close by and bring it swiftly to your attention.

There are times when nasty old Mavis actually brings you down with her and you can end up feeling utterly dejected with life. There are also times she has you seething with anger after having alerted you to something awful. In fact, whenever you pay even the slightest bit of attention to this nasty old witch, you find yourself feeling downright terrible. Why won't she just shut up?

The problem is you pay her rent. You bought nasty old Mavis that chair and you have been putting those words in her mouth. You need to take full responsibility for the fact that you honour old Mavis and her notions; that nobody but you can do anything about her.

You generate all of your own thoughts and have complete control over which ones are digested, which ones are ignored and which ones are cast away immediately. Choose carefully and be responsible. Do not be bullied by negative thoughts. They are yours to control – so become the biggest control freak ever.

Responsibility

As it turns out there's a drop-dead gorgeous woman standing out on a balcony in your mind, warm breeze in her hair, her face (also yours) drinks in the sun. She may not talk as incessantly as nasty old Mavis does, but when she does, she speaks the truth of beauty, acceptance and endless possibilities. Now there's a girl you can listen to.

Responsibility for what comes out of your Mouth

Your WORD is your REALITY!

When I am working one-on-one with clients, it is always interesting to listen to the words they use. Generally, they are unaware of some words that can cause great damage to their lives and prevent them from moving forwards. Breaking the habit of using words that hinder our progress is difficult and something we need to work at doing.

Stephanie's Story

Stephanie was focused on building up her small business and she consistently used the word 'can't' in our conversations. We would discuss fantastic options that could be actioned to propel her towards her goal, but we were inevitably stopped. I drew her attention to the number of times she was using the word 'can't' in our sessions and asked her to examine the effect that this word was having on herself and her life. How can you possibly achieve anything when you consistently tell yourself that you simply can't do it?

Stephanie, like most of us, was completely unaware that she used this damaging word so often but understood the impact it was having. That week, we used a simple technique that would help Stephanie draw her attention to the use of the word 'can't' in her daily life. I asked Stephanie to select a quirky word and she chose the word 'beans'. Then every time Stephanie went to say 'can't', she had to replace it with the word 'beans'.

PUMPED

Stephanie turned up to the next session very surprised. She had been stumbling all week over the word 'beans' as she quickly caught herself about to say the word 'can't'. This is a simple but powerful technique that brought Stephanie's attention to her own speech habit and altered it immediately. Eliminating the word 'can't' from her vocabulary meant that Stephanie was forced to look for alternative solutions – a fast way to see yourself as a woman who 'can'.

Remember, what you focus on is what persists. Words to watch:

- There's **never** enough money.
- It's **too hard** to change careers at my age.
- This is going to be such a **nightmare**.
- I'm **starving**!
- I'm too **scared** to ask.
- I **hate** my bum.
- This is a huge **problem**.
- Things are just so **hectic** at the moment.
- I **should** really do more exercise.
- I **can't** cook to save myself.

Words can make all the difference. A word I stopped using was 'starving'. Whenever I was hungry I would yelp, 'I'm starving!' Can you imagine how my subconscious approached the fridge or a takeaway counter with that statement in mind? I wasn't 'starving' at all. I am fortunate enough to never have been starving, but that was what I was telling myself. In effect, I was ordering very large meals and over-eating because of this one simple statement I was making. Now, saying that I am ready to eat something or that I am a little peckish has me look into the window of that sandwich counter in a whole new way (not to mention the way I look in the mirror!).

Don't underestimate the power of your words. Your subconscious hears the exact words that you speak and turns them into your reality.

Responsibility

Work with your Words

You need to brief someone with this technique, so that they can listen for the negative words you use. Generally, you will find that there are 1 or 2 words that you use consistently, but there is no harm in them picking you up on all of the negative words you use. Brief your partner, a close friend or a work colleague. When you use a negative word, have them repeat it back to you and then you can replace the word with another more positive word and repeat the sentence. This will train you in speaking more positively and break that habit you have formed.

When you discover a negative word you use a lot, replace it with a silly word as Stephanie did. The word must be completely unrelated to the original and something that will sound utterly out of place in the sentence. This will initially train you to not use the 'destructive' word and by using the silly word, all power will be taken out of your negative statements. Experiment with alternative statements that empower you rather than limit you…and stick to them.

My Story

I once reflected on the words I use with my children. 'You're killing me!', 'What is wrong with you?', 'Why are you being so naughty?' Our brains tend to focus on the subject of most sentences, rather than the adjectives and adverbs. Essentially, what my children were hearing were the words 'killing', 'wrong' and 'naughty' in relation to them. In the context of 'what you say creates your reality', is this the reality I was committed to creating? No way!

Responsibility for your Mood

We let ourselves be managed by our moods because we like to think that we cannot control them; that we and our loved ones are well and truly at their mercy. Next time you feel yourself slam the car door, bash the plates in the sink or begin to mutter nasty asides, stop! Take 100% responsibility for the feeling that is manipulating you in that very moment and make the choice to manage it differently.

The fact is, something has happened that has you feeling this way. At this point, it is very powerful to stop for a moment, recognise the feeling for what it is, and make a conscious effort to manage it in a positive way. Nobody enjoys being in or around a negative mood so we must own our disposition and take full responsibility for it. If you make the choice to change your mood in that moment, take action. You may just have to take a walk, listen to some music or play with your children. If you are aware that there are certain triggers which can affect your mood (e.g. being premenstrual, extended work hours, bumping into a long-time nemesis), try to recognise the mood swing as it is taking hold and make a concerted effort to remove yourself from that situation, if possible.

If you find that your mood swings tend to become more frequent or extreme, perhaps it is best to speak to your health care provider for advice.

Alternatively, accept the way you feel and get out of everybody's way. Yes, you have the right to feel angry but only *you* can be responsible for this by not putting yourself in a position where you can upset others.

Everyone will have a different way of disciplining their moods, but using your power to do so is the only way you will feel better about yourself and the people around you. Pick up the responsibility that you threw to the ground during a tantrum years ago and stop letting your mood swings run the show.

'Awesome things will happen today if you choose
not to be a miserable cow.'

-Unknown-

Responsibility

Responsibility for your Perception

We all have a different perspective on things, so it follows that there would be as many perceptions as there are people involved. You are just one person with your own unique set of ideas, beliefs, circumstances and thoughts, and it is important that you realise that. No one will think the same way as you, see a situation the same as you or understand something like you would, so there is a level of responsibility that you need to accept about how you see things differently to others.

We see this often throughout every area in our lives and in society in general; people trying to convince others that their perspective is the right one – on religion, politics, sexual orientation, parenting, career choices, health – I've even had someone try to convince me which is the *best* flavour of ice cream! I mean, seriously!

When you relate to others as being different to you, then you will not need to convince other people of your point of view. You will not need everyone to agree with you because you will understand and accept that is impossible inside of the human experience.

Accepting responsibility that your perception is unlike anyone else's, will give you a greater level of self-acceptance and a significant increase in your confidence. If your perception is simply that, then there's nothing left to prove.

How do you view taking 100% Responsibility for:

- The way your life is turning out?
- Your relationship with your boss?
- How your husband relates to you?
- The parents you have?
- Whether you enjoy your work?
- How someone behaves around you?
- The way your body looks?
- Your health?
- The state of your finances?
- Your career path?
- The fact that you were retrenched?
- Your business?
- That you are busy?
- That you have no relaxation time?
- How the government is behaving?
- If you have been injured?
- The car accident you had last month?
- Your confidence levels?

Responsibility

PUMPED Points to Remember

- Being 100% responsible for every facet of our own lives means harnessing the power to optimise our happiness. Denying full responsibility just means surrendering your own power and becoming the victim of a particular person, situation, thought or feeling. Where is the sense in that?

Take Responsibility for:

- Your current relationships. Are you being 100% responsible or taking the easy road out at 50%, or even 0%?
- Your life goals. An extraordinary life isn't just going to 'happen' to you.
- Your health, weight and fitness – yep, they are all down to you as well.
- Your career.
- Your finances.
- Your time.
- Your view of the world.
- Your frustrations and negativity.
- Your mood.
- Your life!

All yours! Welcome to responsibility and power!

If you take full responsibility for a situation then you are taking power over your ability to respond to it.

It's all an Illusion!

Six

The Illusion of the Wrong Decision

In my experience, one of the biggest fears we have is the fear of making the wrong decision. We get stuck in the dilemma of trying to predict the future, to see what is going to happen and to know which way to turn. It is an impossible situation.

Whenever I feel myself becoming stressed from analysing all the pros and cons, trying desperately to make the 'right' decision, I ask myself one of the most insightful questions I know:

If there was no such thing as a wrong decision and all the options before me were correct, which option would I then choose?

More often than not, there is one option that stands out as my preference when I take away the pressure of finding the 'correct' one.

When I ask people what an increase in confidence will give them, I get many saying that they want the confidence to make the 'right' decision. It is always interesting to see their faces when I tell them that *every* decision they make is the right decision.

I truly believe that the wrong decision is an illusion that we have created and, because it is so handy, we continue to honour its existence. For instance, avoiding the wrong decision is a great excuse for not making a decision at all! Can you imagine if you related to yourself as someone who couldn't make a wrong decision? What excuse would you then have not to make a clear choice and move forward?

The other beautiful thing about having a 'wrong decision' waiting in the wings is that if you decide to take path B, and it doesn't quite go to plan you can always blame yourself and your 'wrong decision'. Clearly, you should have chosen path A – but you didn't.

Let's look at the illusion of the wrong decision more closely. Let's assume you have a choice to make - Path A or Path B. There is no certainty of either outcome, it is only where you 'think' each path is going to take you. Ultimately, everything you imagine is a prediction and you really have no way of knowing where both paths will actually lead you. There are just too many variables. As soon as you decide to go down Path A and you take the first step, Path B disappears as an option and is no longer there. All you are left with is the prediction (that you made up) about where you 'think' Path B may have taken you. Sure, you can consider how things have happened in the past and what you 'think' the pros and cons are, but the truth is, your choices will always be affected by an infinite number of variables, so each new decision will always lead you to a new path. The confidence comes from believing that you've always made the right decision and you can handle anything that comes your way.

Confused yet? Well, hang in there…

So, you start heading down Path A and it doesn't go quite the way you predicted. Perhaps it even becomes the very opposite of what you had originally set out to achieve. You now believe that you have made the wrong decision by choosing Path A. You start fantasising - and remember, it is just a fantasy - about what could have happened if you had chosen what you now consider to be the right decision - Path B. Still with me?

What I want you to realise is that the way Path B was going to go was all made up by you! You like to think you can say for sure what it would have been like, but in truth, it is all just one big imaginative story that you have created. There is every chance that Path B could have left you in a far less desirable situation than Path A. Wouldn't you then have considered Path A to be the right decision?

It's all an Illusion!

Sandra's Story

I started working with Sandra about a year after she had quit her full time role in accounts to open a gift shop in her local area. The gift shop had not done as well as she had hoped in its first year of trading and it looked as though she was going to have to close it down and return to a paid position. Sandra's ideas of what the gift shop life would be like had changed completely from her original plan. Instead of running a beautiful shop full of beautiful things and being happy to go to work every day, Sandra felt immense stress every moment she stood behind that shop counter as she hung on every customer that walked in to make a purchase, just so she could break even.

Sandra was now at a crossroads. She had to decide whether to close the shop and return to full time work or continue to invest some more capital in the marketing of the shop and try and make it a success. However, she was paralysed by this decision process and just couldn't move forward. With such a massive change to Sandra's original plan for building a successful gift shop and better lifestyle for herself, came a massive hit to her confidence in making decisions or knowing what to do next. She was now questioning her intuition and her ability to make the 'right' decision, fearing that she should have never ventured down this small business path in the first place.

Sandra was now completely stopped and was struggling to take any action as her finances withered away. She came to me hoping I would give her the answer of what to do next. Instead, I worked with Sandra on her perspective of the situation and her confidence in making her own decisions and taking action.

Firstly, we discussed that in this instance, she had initially made a decision to leave full time work and open the gift shop (Path A) and, at that time, the alternative was to stay in the full time accounts work she was already employed in (Path B).

PUMPED

Before she made this choice, she imagined that Path A was going to give her a wonderful lifestyle, make her money that would support her, allow her to work in a beautiful shop that she was passionate about and be in charge of her own business. At the same time, she imagined that Path B would allow her to continue to make a steady wage and she was likely to be given a promotion to supervisor once the current supervisor had left. Sandra chose Path A and opened the gift shop.

Now, Sandra was looking back on this decision and regretting that she had chosen Path A instead of Path B. What we worked through was realising that her 'idea' of Path B's outcome was made up. I challenged her to consider that maybe if she had gone with Path B then the supervisor may never have left so she was never going to get that promotion. We also considered that maybe the company was going to hit some tough times and she was likely to be retrenched within a year. Maybe a new manager would have been employed with whom she didn't get on or maybe they would have decided to move the office to a location that was a lot further away for her to travel. Clearly, the 'maybe's' could go on and on and on.

Sandra suddenly started to realise that her ideal of where Path B would have taken her was nothing more than a made up story. It was totally imaginary, something that only *might* have happened but, with all the unconsidered variables, was more than likely *not* to happen. Gradually, the stress of thinking she had made the wrong decision was subsiding and her confidence in herself was trickling back.

Now, another decision was imminent. She had to either close the shop and return to full time work (Path C) or invest more money for marketing in the shop and continue to keep it open (Path D). I asked her, 'Now you know you can't make a wrong decision, what choice do you want to make?'

It's all an Illusion!

Sandra decided to invest more money and continue her beautiful gift shop for another 6 months, at which time she would make another decision on whether to stay open or not. However, the main breakthrough was that Sandra now had a whole new sense of freedom around the gift shop, her ability to make decisions and her confidence and belief in herself. She can choose the path she wants to take and go down it confidently with no regrets. Now that's freedom!

From this story we can see how futile it is to regret any choices you have made in your life, as it is impossible to ever know how the other alternatives would have turned out.

This can be a tough concept to grasp so read it again until you get it. It is an extremely valuable perception that will have you completely free to move forward easily in your life and have confidence with the choices you make. It will also allow you to have confidence in the choices you have already made in your life no matter what they were. Consider that every choice you have made in the past has taught you the lessons you needed to learn, introduced you to the people you needed to meet and given you the insights you needed to gain, in order to have you equipped to take on the future.

The Illusion of Reality

> 'Two men look out the same prison bars;
> one sees mud and the other stars.'
>
> -Rev. Frederick Langbridge-

Reality is only what our perception allows us to accept as being real. We have already discussed that there are as many perspectives as there are people involved. So, reality is different for all of us.

PUMPED

Communication is the key to training our minds to see things from others' points of view. Really listening to people allows you to gain insights into their perspective and to try and understand its variation from yours. Our brains work by making connections to neural hardwiring it already knows and understands. For example, both you and I may be standing together and we see a dog coming towards us. My brain sees the dog and makes a connection to my own dog that I love. Whereas your brain connects it to an incident a few years ago when you were bitten by a dog. We are both experiencing the same situation but our perspective on it can be vastly different.

Changing our perception is also a matter of paying close attention to your automatic responses and actively searching for other ways to see the situation. If your perception is not doing you any justice, and if all you see is the 'mud', then you must train yourself to look for the 'stars'.

Your interpretation of reality will have a significant impact on your confidence and your life. Imagine that 2 women in the same job role of a company were retrenched on the same day (essentially the same reality). Woman 1 is devastated. She tells everyone how terrible this situation is, that she will never recover, that the job market is so tough and how she will likely be out of work for months - Mud.

Woman 2 is initially a bit shaken by the sudden change in plans, however, she decides that this is a great opportunity for her to take a new direction. She tells everyone that the retrenchment is going to bring her amazing opportunities; that she is looking forward to seeing what else is out there in the job market and whether she can get something that pays more and is closer to home. She decides to make this the best thing that has ever happened to her and enjoy some much needed time off while she looks for the perfect job - Stars.

Regardless of the individuals' circumstances, which woman do you think will have the best chance of being employed in a wonderful new job? Woman 2, of course. Woman 1 is going to spend so much energy being stuck in the mud that she's unlikely to be open to any wonderful new job opportunity that may come her way.

Perspective of our reality can be affected by a number of factors - history, values, attitudes and circumstance, just to name a few. A tendency to have a pessimistic or optimistic view of our reality may come as a consequence of a background that has taught us that this particular attitude is necessary for our protection and survival. Remember, the choice is always there to be optimistic, to focus on the wonderful people in the world, to seek out the positive in every instance and to squeeze the utmost joy out of life. Make your choice - the beauty of your reality is entirely in your hands.

The Illusion of Failure

Failure? There is no such thing. What is often perceived as a failure is actually just a temporary setback, roadblock or an unexpected detour.

Can you truly accept this statement or did you just want to skip this section and move on? I once thought I truly recognised that there was no such thing as failure until one day I heard the words 'I don't want to fail' come out of my mouth. Now, if I had really believed there was no such thing as failure then I wouldn't be afraid of it, would I? So I started some research into the topic to find out the truth once and for all.

The more I read, the more I realised that failure is indeed just a word and not a reality at all. When you do not achieve a desired outcome, it is not a failure, it is a result. Ok, so it may not be the result you aimed for, but it is still a result.

As we start along the path to achieving certain goals in life there is one thing that you can absolutely guarantee – there are going to be a few bumps and detours along the way. These are not, however, signs of impending failure.

'Giving up on a goal because of a setback, is like slashing your other 3 tires because you got a flat.'

-Unknown-

For instance, if you are driving to a particular destination and you come across a detour, do you consider that you have failed on your journey and turn around? No, of course not! You take the detour and keep going. Sure, you may have had to change direction for a while but, by keeping focused on the original destination, you eventually make it there. And in most cases, you travel along a route that is new and interesting; it may offer a much better view and even get you to your destination sooner.

Why is this any different from the journeys we make to specific destinations in our lives? (Note: I use the word 'specific' here because if you do not have a specific destination in mind, you will never know when or if you ever get there!) To increase confidence, it is vital that we change our perception of failure. If we don't, any little bump or detour in the road will stop us in our tracks and, if you consider that the only thing you can absolutely guarantee is that you will come across bumps and detours, then it could be impossible for you to ever reach your destination!

Also, it will no doubt limit the endeavours you set for yourself because you will still be under the impression that failure is something to be frightened of. It's a little bit like the bogeyman when you are a child; he doesn't really exist but you scare yourself silly over him, spend your nights awake listening for him, avoid going to the bathroom in case he's behind the door and jump straight into your parents' bed when you hear the slightest hint of a footstep.

It's all an Illusion!

Turn on the lights and check under the bed – failure is absolutely nowhere to be seen. So relax and start planning all the things you can do, now that you know nothing is going to get you. That bogeyman is gone for good!

Is Failure an Excuse?

We also use the 'possibility of failure' as an excuse for not doing things - that is why we keep it in existence and we love it. Many people blindly accept that failure is real and that it is something that nobody likes to experience. Your excuse therefore, for not doing something, is totally acceptable to them. They understand and don't challenge you, generally because there are things they too are not doing in their lives because they are scared to fail. (Note that you would never get this sort of acceptance if you were speaking to me!)

If failure didn't exist, if there was really no such thing as failure, we would not be able to use it as an excuse and no one would accept it from us. It would be like saying – 'Oh, I can't do that or try that because, if I did, the sky might fall down on me.' If someone gave you this excuse for not doing something, there is no way you would accept it. Failure is the same. Don't accept that it is real and don't use it as an excuse for a minute longer. It is holding you back from an unbelievably amazing life!

Consider this interaction between 2 friends: the first is an example of accepting failure; the second is when failure is not accepted as an excuse.

Mary: 'I hate my job. There's no way I can find a new one. My life is in such chaos at the moment. I'd better wait until my husband's work situation changes and the kids are at school before I change anything. I don't want to risk it being an even worse situation than it is now.'

Jane's Response Example 1: 'Yeah, it's better the devil you know. No point adding more chaos to your life by job hunting.'

Jane's Response Example 2: 'Well, you've got nothing to lose. Think of how many hours you spend at work. You deserve to be happy. There's no such thing as 'perfect' timing – take control of your happiness and go find a new job!'

'Life's real failure is when you do not realise how close you were to success when you gave up.'

-Thomas A. Edison-

The Crystal Ball Factor

Neither you nor I can be absolutely certain of what the future holds. The events of the next year, the next month, tomorrow or a moment from now are all yet to be seen. We like to think we know what is going to happen because it makes us feel secure but, I'm afraid, security is an illusion too!

I call this the Crystal Ball Factor because we love to try to peer into it and hope to see the future.

My Crystal Ball Story

In the second year of my business, I carried forward a tax debt from the first year of $3,000 which the tax department kindly gave me a year to pay. No sweat! And I was right; I didn't sweat over it at all in the year that followed. I worked hard building the business, ploughed money back into it and spent the profits (well, a girl has to have shoes!).

It wasn't until after New Year had arrived that I pulled the paperwork out and realised that 22nd March was the deadline for the

It's all an Illusion!

$3,000. My blood pressure rose. The beginning of the year was not my busiest time and I was going to find it a huge challenge to come up with the money in time. Soon the recurring image of a small balding tax man, wearing a suit, spectacles and waving a $3,000 bill began to make me very nervous. This was going to be interesting.

It wasn't until the beginning of March that I was able to put some money away towards the debt... 22 days and counting. And with the financial commitments I had ahead of me, it seemed like my 'no sweat' $3,000 was going to have me drowning in perspiration.

Then, things took a turn for the worse! Sitting at a set of traffic lights on a regular Thursday morning, a lady in a very large 4WD put her foot on the accelerator without realising that nobody else was moving and squashed the back of my car like a cola can. My car was an instant write-off; I burst into tears as I envisioned that the insurance company was probably only going to give me a pittance for it and I didn't have any savings to buy myself another car. Plus, there was that looming tax bill!

That was it. Before I could even get out of the car, I had lost all sense of reasonableness and dived headfirst into a state of drama and tragedy that there seemed to be no way out from. My Crystal Ball had surfaced and was flashing neon at me: 'Impending Doom'. Good old Mavis (the negative chatter box) saw that I was vulnerable too and couldn't help herself. She started on me with her non-stop negative nagging, rocking furiously in her chair and giving me a multitude of other reasons to worry. I exploded into a rage of doubt and fear.

'Now I won't be able to pay the taxman at all, let alone buy another car. How am I going to run the business without a car? I won't even be able to see my clients. This is way too much...I can't do this anymore...I'm going backwards financially...I'll have to go back to a regular full-time job...my dream of running my own business is over.'

I was a mess. I had gone to that irrational place where there was nothing that anyone could say to console me, and nasty old Mavis was on red-alert; nothing positive was going to get through. Everyone was just so glad I wasn't hurt, but that was not even on my radar – I wasn't thinking about narrowly escaped broken bones, I was thinking about bankruptcy!

The next day I was still wailing when one of the important souls in my life gave me the perspective I needed and he gave it to me straight:

'If you were injured and in hospital you wouldn't be able to see your clients either. It's time to stand up, shake off the shock and be thankful that it was only the car that was written off. You are still the same determined, inspiring woman you were 2 days ago, it's just that now you don't have a car – and that's it! Everything will be okay, you know that, so pull yourself together and get on with it.'

I realised that I had walked to the edge of the ring, ready to wave my white towel but thankfully, my supporters were there to stop me. I had temporarily lost all my confidence in what I was doing and the belief that I could handle anything that came my way. For the next few days, I went straight back to my confidence program and became religious about saying my favourite, and most powerful, affirmation:

'Everything is working out perfectly.
Everything happens for a reason.
I hand over trust.'

Four days later the insurance company rang me to let me know that there was a problem with my insurance. 'Oh yeah, I need this!' I thought. However, the voice on the other end of the phone chattered at me for a while until my brows were knitted together in confusion.

'What does all that mean?' I asked, eyes shut tight, bracing myself for devastation.

It's all an Illusion!

'It means that an error was made on your insurance and you have been paying too much on your monthly premiums. We are, therefore, obliged to pay you a substantial amount of money in return.'

The insurance company ended up paying me a sum of money many times more than what my broken little car was worth – with the final payment coming through on (yep, you guessed it!) Monday, the 22nd of March. As the payment arrived in my account, I immediately transferred the full $3,000 to the tax department and the rest was enough to buy me a car. Whoa!

I could never have predicted how this story was going to end. I could never have envisaged how I would find $3,000, just as I was never going to be able to forecast the journey of running my own business when I made the decision to do it. The Crystal Ball I kept trying to see the future in, was seriously unreliable! You just have to keep reminding yourself of your destination, take it a step at a time and keep your confidence up. Sure, you can estimate how it might look and set some goals but, ultimately, you will never have a guarantee on what the journey will look like or how many detours there will be on the way.

'Worry is interest paid in advance for a debt you may never owe.'

-Chinese Proverb-

Do not delude or frighten yourself with predictions. It all comes down to that old adage we were told as children - and that you may very well tell your own children – 'you'll never know unless you try'. Put life to the test. It's an adventure that will make you better, stronger, fuller!

PUMPED Points to Remember

- Don't torture yourself with worry over making the wrong decision. It doesn't exist. Check out all the options before you and just make a choice. Then walk forward and never look back!
- Your reality is not my reality. Our perception of facts impacts what we know to be true for us.
- Don't be stopped by the fear of failure. If you start accepting that there is no such thing as failure, you will be able to take on anything you want.
- Stop peering into your Crystal Ball trying to predict the future. This wastes so much time and energy.

Don't regret any choices you make, it is impossible to ever know how the other alternatives would have turned out.

3 Clicks and You're Home

Seven

*'If I ever go looking for my heart's desire again,
I won't look any further than my own backyard...'*

-Dorothy, The Wizard of Oz-

I love the movie The Wizard of Oz (and perhaps this explains my infatuation with red shoes!). It is the tale of Dorothy, our innocent heroine, who finds herself on a magical adventure in the land of Oz, trying desperately to find her way back home to Kansas.

The messages in this movie are deeper than I could have ever related to as a young girl, infatuated only with the pair of sparkly red shoes on the screen. The story along the Yellow Brick Road is one where we encounter a whole host of interesting characters that, if you look beyond the surface, seem to represent so many of our own fears.

Who do you identify with? Are you the Scarecrow who believes he's a failure because he doesn't have a brain, feeling inferior to all others? Can you relate perhaps to the Tin Man who feels sad because he doesn't have a heart, not trusting your feelings and instincts? Maybe you feel like the Lion who puts on a brave roar and scares off intruders but who, deep down, thinks that he doesn't have the courage or power to succeed? The Wizard is also a familiar character – a big fake front with lots of smoke and fire to show his importance and power, but ultimately to hide a very lonely and fearful person.

Oh, and we can't forget Dorothy, who is lost and feels like an alien in this strange land. She is being chased by a wicked witch (guilt, the past, fear?) and spends her whole time trying to find her way home.

Dorothy assumes that somebody else, namely the Wizard, has all the answers for her when really, she has the power to get home all along. It's as easy as just 3 heel clicks of her ruby red slippers!

So, why am I rambling on about an old movie? Well, the message in The Wizard of Oz is the same one I have for you in this book. *You*, my friend, have everything you think you lack; there is simply no need to look outside yourself for the answers.

Inside you lives 100% confidence – it is just a matter of tapping into it and allowing that confidence to flow. That's what the confidence techniques in this book are designed to achieve. Looking outside yourself for affirmation and self-belief is hopeless. Scrambling for reinforcement from others, making dramatic changes to our bodies and comparing ourselves to everybody else gets us no closer to the real essence of confidence. Why? Well, because confidence has lived inside us all along; we cannot obtain it from the outside. It turns out that we had never lost it in the first place; we've just been looking for self-love in all the wrong places.

Never Give In!

'Success is hanging on when you want to let go.'

-Unknown-

And you'll want to let go!

Believe me, I have wanted to let go of many things when the going got tough, but letting go was never going to get me anywhere. When you are clinging to the edge of something, fingernails breaking and knuckles turning white, the battle to stay where you are can become all too much. When the desire to let go overcomes you, stay strong and see the lapse in power for what it really is – a challenge to be overcome.

Becoming a woman with confidence will naturally take some time and effort, and it is guaranteed that your motivation and focus are going to waver from time to time. Remind yourself constantly what you are striving for and that the confidence you also strive for is just around the corner. It's about making it over the hurdles, finding the time to reflect, silencing the excuses and continually acknowledging your efforts. The mere act of making it this far in the book shows that you have made a commitment to live the best life possible and you know that means having the confidence to do what you want with your life.

Although my own quest for confidence stalls at times, I always collect myself and return to my confidence program and the confidence techniques that are tried and tested. You see I know they work, I know what a difference they make to my life and I know that being a confident woman allows me to live a life of freedom, happiness and full self-expression. It allows me to make the most of opportunities, stand up for what I believe in and walk forward in the face of fear. Confidence gives me the ability to follow my dreams, even when nobody else believes they can happen, and take on the very best of what this world has to offer. Who doesn't want that?

My Giving In Story

I had a massive hit to my confidence when I had my children. All of a sudden I moved from a corporate position - where I was listened to, was a valued member of management teams, was looked up to by my staff, wore nice suits and was paid - to a life where I had 2 toddlers who never listened to me, where my daily role was now cleaning up nappies and mashed food; I wore t-shirts and shorts that were also stained from the mashed food, I didn't get paid for my 16 hour days and the only staff member that looked up to me was my washing machine as I shoved piles of clothes down its throat daily! It was a big lifestyle change and at times it was very challenging to maintain my self-worth and confidence while I had squished banana hanging out of my hair.

I felt like giving up.

Once again, I got myself back on track with the confidence techniques that I knew worked for me, and which brought me back to life. As your life changes shape your confidence program will always be there to pull you through – you just have to get back in touch with the techniques that work for you and rediscover the woman that you truly are.

So, when your old habits start to reappear, your life changes dramatically or your motivation wavers, just remember it is a natural part of the journey. It's that roller coaster ride we talked about at the beginning of the book. Ride the rollercoaster car down but just never get out. It's up to you to turn that downward ride upward again and now you are learning the tools to do exactly that!

No Low Flying Ducks!

As you start on your way to conquering your world, beware of what I call, the 'Low Flying Duck Syndrome'. This is when people, who are achieving wonderful and incredible things in their lives, fly 'below the pack'. You may know it better as flying below the radar or avoiding tall poppy syndrome. Regardless of the title, it refers to people who are concerned about making others feel substandard or being seen to have an ego problem, so they choose to fly lower than they really should. They don't share their successes with others, they keep the things they are proud of to themselves and they downplay their achievements and acknowledgements.

Well, let me tell you something: Low Flying Ducks are no good to anyone. It's an illusion that withholding your achievements and undervaluing your progress will allow others to feel better. Conversely, it is those who dare to step up and take life on who are inspirations to all others. Those who work hard, fight through fear and achieve their dreams are people that the rest of us look towards in awe.

3 Clicks and You're Home

Imagine if an Olympic athlete, who had worked hard to achieve their goal for many years, finally won their race and then refused to stand on the podium because they were concerned that they might make the crowd feel second-rate. It just doesn't happen, does it? They take the top step of that podium with pride and hold their heads high for all to see. We in the crowd are inspired by what these amazing athletes achieve. If you're anything like me, you become instantly uplifted by this testimony, reminding us that if you train hard, you really can accomplish these astounding achievements.

As you start to use the techniques and feel their affects, stand tall on that podium of confidence. Be somebody that leads by example and gives others the strength, courage, motivation and guts to love who they are, live self-expressed and be free. You will have the power and ability to inspire the people around you, and that is a gift worth giving!

Don't fly low, soar high, so the rest of us can follow!

'The eagle likes to fly high above the world, not to look down on people but to encourage them to look up.'

-Unknown-

Inside you lives
100% confidence.
You already have
everything you need.
It is just a matter of
tapping into it and allowing
that confidence to flow.

PART 2

GET PUMPED!
BE CONFIDENT!

Designing your own Personal Confidence Program

Get Pumped! Be Confident!

Think of your Personal Confidence Program like a healthy eating or exercise plan. If you want a healthy body then you know that you must follow a healthy eating and exercise plan that works for you. You can't just eat one carrot or do one push-up and hope that you've done enough.

Confidence is no different. As we have already discussed, it wavers all the time. Sometimes you will feel amazingly confident and then it will change and you will feel fear, doubt, low self-belief and low self-worth. If you have a proven Confidence Program in place, one that you implement consistently, then the lows will quickly turn around to highs again.

So, work through the techniques listed here. Don't just try them once but implement them into your daily life and see the changes start to take place. Over time, you will have a short list of the techniques that really work for you. These will start to form the basis of your Personal Confidence Program that you will use for life.

This part of the book is split into 3 sections:

1. **THINK** Confidently – these techniques will help you change your attitude and the way the thoughts in your head speak to you;

2. **ACT** Confidently – these techniques will assist you to both *appear* more confident and *be* more confident in your daily life;

3. **LIVE** Confidently – these techniques will help you shape your environment so you have positive influences around you that support living as a confident woman.

THINK Confidently!

> 'Thought is the sculptor who can create the person you want to be.'
>
> -Henry David Thoreau-

Let's review some key points:

Confidence is an attitude and that attitude originates in your thoughts. Whatever else you decide to do, the most critical step to increasing your confidence is changing your thoughts.

Everything starts with a thought.

Nothing exists before the thought exists.

Nothing can become reality until you have the thought that it can.

As your thinking changes, your outer reality changes too. It's the thoughts you think that create your life. Your thoughts are creative and create your experiences.

Positive, optimistic thoughts = positive, optimistic experiences and events.

Happy, successful thoughts = a happy, successful life.

Confident thoughts = a confident life.

The techniques below are simple although sometimes challenging. But they are the most effective for becoming a confident woman. Your head rules your life, what you say to yourself creates your world and every thought you think has an impact on who you are.

Acknowledgement Diary

This is a wonderful technique, which will ensure you change the way you see your life within days. Hello confidence!

Buy yourself a small diary that you can keep next to your bed. Before you go to sleep *every night* write a personal acknowledgment in that diary. Record something that you did that day of which you were proud. Some examples might be:

- I acknowledge myself for getting out of bed and going for a walk this morning when I really didn't want to.
- Today I want to acknowledge myself for speaking out at the meeting.
- I am proud of myself for helping out a friend today.
- I acknowledge myself for being patient with the kids all day.
- I acknowledge myself for ensuring I got some 'Me Time' today.
- Good on me for volunteering to be the coordinator of the committee.

It can be as big or as small as you like - just be sure to write something in it each and every night.

You might find this a little difficult at first, especially if you have a raving internal critic.

Trish's Story

One of the clients I worked with, Trish, was really down on herself. We arranged for her to email me every night with an acknowledgement for that day. On the first day, she sat in front of that computer for an hour before she could find something in her day she wanted to write about. Her focus on being proud of herself was way off. The next day, she sat there for another hour, however, as the week progressed, she started to take note during the day of things she felt good about so she could write them in the email to me that night. We continued

THINK Confidently!

this technique in the form of daily emails for nearly 3 weeks before the acknowledgments started to flow more easily for her.

Generally, we default to focusing on the things we didn't do and the things we might have done better. We may even be beating ourselves up about something we did 'wrong' today or even something we did last week. The Acknowledgement Diary forces you to refocus your self-perception. Knowing you have to give yourself an acknowledgment at the end of every day means you are soon taking special note of your wins and things you feel good about, giving you a completely different perspective on your day and yourself. You will feel the benefits instantly, I promise!

WOW Book

'Self-doubt is the anchor that keeps our ships from sailing.'

-Unknown-

Self-doubt will continue to torment us until the end of time. The secret is managing it.

I have had a WOW book for many years and this is a technique I have used with many clients who were struggling to get their self-doubt under control. What you will need is a notebook of some description. Some clients prefer a small one that will fit in their handbag, others have bought larger ones to sit on their desk and some have bought large sketchpads to work in. It is really up to you what you want your WOW book to look like and you can be as creative as you like. This book then becomes a record for all those moments that make you say 'Wow!'

Moments like these:

- 'Wow, that was such an amazing thing they said about me.'
- 'Wow, what an encouraging email.'

- 'Wow, what a flattering compliment!'
- 'Wow, what fantastic feedback.'
- 'Wow, I am so proud that I did that.'
- 'Wow, I have just received my first cheque in my new business.'
- 'Wow, I achieved my goal of ….'

Actively seek out additions to your WOW Book. Write down the compliment someone gave you, stick a copy of a great email in or make a note of what someone else said about you that was awesome. Soon, you will have a wonderful book full of acknowledgments, compliments and proud moments that are otherwise easily forgotten. Whenever you're feeling scared, doubtful or fearful, you can read the entries in this book to get you back in touch with the reality of how other people see you. You spend far too much time with yourself to have a clear perspective on who you are and what you are capable of. The WOW book entries are who you *really* are!

Extra Note: This is a wonderful technique to use inside your relationship. Create a small 'WOW Book of Love' and enter into it all those things that your partner does to show their love (both big and small). It is all too easy for us to forget those tender moments (especially when they leave their wet towel on the floor or forget to take the bins out), so create a book specifically for that. Then you'll have a wonderful reminder of the special text messages, little notes, cards and those comments that really touched your heart.

Affirmations

We have discussed affirmations at length in the earlier chapters so now it's time to just do them! Affirmations change the negative voice in your head that has been telling you for years that you are no good, that you're stupid or that you can't do it. You have to stop that voice to achieve the levels of confidence you seek and the best way to do that is to repeat positive statements constantly.

THINK Confidently!

And I mean constantly! Constant repetition is the only way to overwrite the negative recording that's been playing in your head for years. Your subconscious mind doesn't have a sense of humour. It takes the thoughts from your conscious mind as the instruction for the outcomes you wish to produce. Your subconscious mind works continuously to bring your dominant thoughts to fruition. If it has been programmed with negative, low confidence, disempowering thoughts, then it's time to turn that around!

The balance of power between the negative and the positive can only be shifted if the old, worn and disempowering thoughts are replaced with new encouraging ones. Think of your many years' worth of negative thoughts to be an old, cracked and dilapidated building with weak foundations. In the face of an earthquake (a.k.a. a life challenge or crisis), there's a good chance that building will crumble down around you. If you want to give yourself the best chance of a great penthouse view though, you need to build the strongest foundations possible and use the best construction materials available to you. And what better materials to use than confidence, encouragement and positivity in the form of continuous affirmations? Yes, the building may shake occasionally if the earth trembles, but its strength will ensure it always stays upright and you'll always be safe.

The most powerful way to do this is to speak those affirmations out loud to yourself. This may not be possible when you are sitting on a crowded train going to work (well you can, you might just get a lot of sidewards glances). Therefore, there are a number of ways to do them (it doesn't matter which one you pick as long as you pick one);

1. Speak positive statements aloud (great for driving alone in the car).
2. Repeat positive statements in your head, silently over and over.
3. Write positive statements down, over and over and over.
4. Record yourself saying the positive statements and play them over and over.

Regular repetition is the key here. Set up your environment to help you – have your positive statements on the fridge, on your computer, in your diary, attached to your car keys or behind the toilet door! It doesn't really matter where or when you do them, what is important is that you DO them, over and over and over and over and over...

My Affirmation Story

I remember when I was working in the corporate world, I would repeat my affirmations in time with my steps as I walked to and from the train station and to and from work. This became a daily ritual and really set me in a positive mood for the day. Now I repeat them a lot when I exercise or go for a walk. Again, when I am in the rhythm of a good walk the positive statements seem to easily fit.

I also regularly read '*You Can Heal Your Life*' by Louise L. Hay. I pick it up and read it a few times every year and it helps remind me of the importance of continuing the affirmations in my life. I also have a number of affirmation cards on my desk that I can use to quickly re-focus. Having these wonderful statements on hand can really turn the day around if needed.

Eliminate Self-Hate Behaviours

Take a sheet of paper and divide the page into 2 columns: Self-Love and Self-Hate. Next, look carefully at your life and at all the different behaviours you exhibit. As you recognise each behaviour decide whether each is born out of self-love or self-hate and add it to the relevant column.

Acknowledging the behaviours you have listed in the Self-Hate section is an enormous step towards eliminating them from your life. Be consistently mindful of the destructive things you put yourself through and teach yourself not to do it. Replace the behaviours that are detrimental to your happiness with self-affirming habits and you will look fantastic, feel incredible and begin to see yourself in a whole new (more flattering) light. Revel in it.

For a list of possible Self-Love and Self-Hate behaviours, review our 'Accepting You' section earlier in the book.

Manage Fear

The best way to manage your fear is to firstly accept that fear as a natural part of your life and, secondly, to do the thing that you fear the most. As we have explored earlier, you need to get comfortable with being uncomfortable.

Start small, but just get started today. Do something today that you fear. Anything! Maybe it's making a phone call you have been putting off, applying for a promotion or making the effort to sit with a different group of people over lunch at work. You could speak up at a meeting, wear something that draws attention to you or continue singing loudly when you stop the car at the lights (yes, while people are watching!).

Take out some paper and write down a list of things you would love to do but are too afraid to try. Write a long list of everything you can think of and then get busy.

In My Opinion!

Do you realise how many opinions you have? There are literally millions of them. You have opinions about your life, your society, the way the country is run, how your friend should deal with her problem or even which career your children should have. We form opinions about almost everything and are creating them moment-by-moment, day after day, year in, year out! When you consider that most opinions are unsubstantiated by any real knowledge or proof, we have to question the opinions we hold or that we accept from others.

It is incredibly easy to form an opinion. Most of us only have to look at a book cover and instantly we form an opinion as to whether we're going to like it or not. Unfortunately, most of us do the same just by looking at another person too. Just their appearance can have us form an opinion of them. Research suggests that when meeting someone it only takes 6 seconds before an opinion of them is formed. Only 6 seconds before we've read the book by its cover!

You see, the problem with opinions is that everybody's got one. We have opinions about everything, even about things we simply know nothing about. I know I've imparted my opinion more than a few times about a topic I know little to nothing about. I can take a little bit of information and have an elaborate and convincing conversation - can't you?

The point I'm trying to make here is that we must all be extremely careful whose opinions we listen to. Too many of us hear someone's opinion and accept it as the truth. This is so easily done and so totally ridiculous when you consider how unfounded most opinions are. Look at how bombarded we are daily with a multitude of opinions – we read articles, watch the news, buy magazines and absorb massive amounts of online information. How else would celebrity endorsements work so well?

I clearly remember my 3rd grade teacher telling me that I wasn't good at spelling when I messed up on a test. It was a view that I considered to be the truth for many years, until I realised that it was just *her* opinion and that it wasn't even founded on much evidence. She had once made a quick statement and I had believed those words for years.

Julie's Story

I was once working with a client named Julie who told me quite convincingly that the particular job that she was looking for was very difficult to find.

'Really?' I asked. 'How do you know that?'
'Oh, my friend told me,' she said.

THINK Confidently!

'And how does your friend know this?'

'Oh, she read something about this industry a few months back,' was her reply.

I challenged this opinion and my client found out personally that, in fact, there were many positions that she was looking for currently being advertised. Her friend had formed an opinion from something she'd read (which turned out to be just someone else's opinion) and had taken it to be the truth. This incorrect belief was preventing her from leaving her current position that she was terribly unhappy in. She changed her belief because she realised that the opinion she had taken as truth was totally unfounded and went on to get herself a great new job!

Opinions are not always negative but it is the negative ones that seem to be easier to accept and consequently cause us the most harm. Someone once said Richard Branson would never amount to anything because he didn't finish school…an opinion that has proven to be totally off the mark. Seeing as the man has achieved enormous feats over the years and is currently trying to fly passengers into space, it would be totally foolish for anyone to doubt Richard Branson's ability to achieve something!

People are free to say what they like but it is up to us to decipher what we will believe. Once we accept someone's opinion as the truth, it gives that opinion power and validity. This is why we must be extremely cautious with what opinions we choose to accept and take on as the truth. My tip would be to only believe what empowers you and forget the rest.

Consider which opinions you have taken on as the truth that may not be serving you. Many of them may be difficult to find, as you have probably believed them for so long that you have forgotten that it was just someone's unfounded opinion that you accepted a long time ago. However, it is important to challenge your beliefs constantly. If you think you can't do something, ask yourself why and what hard evidence you have for that view. I guarantee that most of the limits we place on ourselves have no real evidence or truth to them – just another little unfounded opinion! Challenge them all and change the way you see your world.

The technique here is to place the words 'In My Opinion...' before anything anybody says to you - especially anything negative, pessimistic or unsupportive. If you can master this, you will be able to prevent people's opinions automatically entering your consciousness as the truth. This is immensely powerful and allows you to stop the disempowering opinions people give you at the door!

Let's see it in action:

Your colleague says: 'You're not ready for that promotion.'

Sounds definitive, doesn't it?

Now let's try it this way. In your head, repeat what they have said with my prefix in front of it: 'In my opinion, you're not ready for that promotion.' Doesn't have as much power, does it? Especially if we don't really respect that person's opinions!

Let's try some more:
- '**In My Opinion**... this government is hopeless.'
- '**In My Opinion**... my child is gifted and talented.'
- '**In My Opinion**... you're not really going to stick with that exercise plan.'
- '**In My Opinion**... you're good, but you're not that good.'
- '**In My Opinion**... that's too complicated.'
- '**In My Opinion**... that's not going to work.'
- '**In My Opinion**... you'll go to hell for that.'
- '**In My Opinion**... that's the best school to send your child to.'
- '**In My Opinion**... you'll never find the time to do that.'
- '**In My Opinion**... that's right/wrong/easy/hard/boring/exciting.'

Use this for EVERYONE – yes, your parents, your sister, your best friend, your husband, your coach, your teacher, your mentor, your boss, your religious leader, your wealthy friend, the politicians, your favourite lead singer, your colleagues, your industry leaders, the mothers in your playgroup or at the school gate... everyone. It's not that you are going to disagree with everything they are saying, you just want to prevent what they say from being automatically taken as the truth. Their opinions only have power if *you* believe them. Find out more for yourself and question the status quo. It might just transform your life.

Ditch the Disempowering Thoughts

Speaking of other people's opinions, how many from the past have you taken on as the truth? Sometimes these beliefs were adopted so long ago that we are not even consciously aware of it.

It's time to ditch the disempowering thoughts, regardless of where they came from. They are not serving you and they are definitely doing you and your life incredible amounts of harm.

If you were ever told that you're stupid;
They were wrong!
If you were ever told you're hopeless;
They were wrong!
If you were ever told that you're ugly;
They were wrong!
If you were ever told that you're a failure;
Darling, they were wrong!
If you were ever told that you're a disappointment;
They too were wrong!
If you have ever been told you were bad, awful, clueless, a disgrace, dumb, horrible, inferior, insignificant, retarded, unworthy, unimportant, unlovable, unwanted or worthless;
They (whoever they are) were absolutely and totally wrong, wrong, wrong! It was an opinion they voiced that you believed.

Don't believe the lies for another single second.

Worry Less About What Others Think

> 'You wouldn't care what people thought of you
> if you realised how seldom they do.'
>
> -Chinese Proverb-

This is an important mind shift to grasp for your confidence. So many people I speak to are overly concerned with what others think of them and this seems especially true for women. What will 'they' think of me, of my clothes, of my children, of my business, of my decisions and of my life? Not to mention my hair, my big ass, how old I look, what car I drive, the suburb I live in or whether this dress suits me or not?

The mind shift is...ready for it...

THEY ARE NOT THINKING ABOUT YOU BECAUSE THEY ARE TOO BUSY THINKING ABOUT THEMSELVES AND WHAT OTHERS ARE THINKING OF THEM!

Ok, I know that was loud but it was supposed to be. When you can really get this, you can really start to worry a whole lot less about what others are thinking of you (because they're not) and just get on with your life. The irony is that *you* are being stopped from doing something because of what people might think but these people are stopped from doing things also because of what *you* might think. RIDICULOUS! Everyone is stopped, not living the lives or doing the things they want, not being the person they really are, (and probably whinging about it all) because they are so concerned about what 'others' are thinking.

OK, here comes the shouting again...

NOBODY REALLY CARES!

THINK Confidently!

I'm sorry to burst your bubble but nobody really cares too much about what you are up to, what you are wearing or how much weight you have put on. It's natural that a thought will pass through their heads about your dress, your kids, your car, your partner or your hair but they move through that thought pretty darn quickly because they are having the same conversation in their head about what others think about *their* dress, *their* kids, *their* car, *their* partner and yes, *their* hair too. THAT'S what they are really concerned with – THEMSELVES – NOT YOU!

Isn't that a relief?

They are not concerned with you as much as you think they are.

They don't really care.

Now, get on with your life!

Your PUMPED Action Plan

- Start to acknowledge yourself in writing every day. No, just thinking it is not enough. Write it down and do it every day. Keep yourself accountable and do this technique with a trusted friend. Make a rule that you must email or text each other your acknowledgement each and every day. If someone forgets, they buy lunch!
- Create a WOW book today and start filling it. This is really who you are in the world.
- DO your positive affirmations. Not maybe, not tomorrow, not half-heartedly - do them today and reap the immediate rewards. When you have a healthy, positive, powerful and encouraging mind, life works and everything is available to you. The alternative is to waste your amazing life and potential.
- Eliminate self-hate behaviours. Get your list and focus on **not** doing one each week. Go get that amazing self-love stuff!
- Learn about dealing with fear. Read books, take a course – whatever floats your boat! Dealing with fear will be the BEST lesson you'll ever learn.
- Challenge your current beliefs and be extremely careful whose opinions you are listening to. People's negative opinions are generally unfounded, unproductive and downright damaging.
- Remember - they are not thinking about you because they are too busy thinking about themselves. Get over it!

Be extremely careful whose opinions you are listening to. People's negative opinions are generally unfounded, unproductive and downright damaging.

ACT Confidently!

Acting like a confident woman shows the world that this is now who you are. I love the old saying 'You teach people how to treat you' so by acting like a confident woman, people will begin to treat you like one.

This section shares with you some confidence techniques to ensure you act like a confident woman!

Fake It Till You Make It

Even if (and especially if) you don't feel confident on the inside, it is important to show confidence on the outside. Sometimes you just need to 'fake it till you make it' and generally, you will find that the act of faking it actually helps you to make it.

'What we think, we become.'

-Buddha-

The outside world really does take you at your own estimate. Usually, I am an outwardly confident woman so I am generally treated as such by the outside world. What I mean by this is that I have noticed the difference in the way some people will treat me as opposed to others around me who don't show or speak with the same amount of confidence.

My Confidence Story

I was in a clothing store, 3 deep in a line waiting to pay when I could hear the woman at the front of the line timidly start speaking to the sales lady. She had her head down, her eyes down and spoke with a soft mumble that was almost too hard to hear. The sales lady asked her to repeat herself as she tried to understand what the lady was after but, as the conversation went on, you could visibly see the sales lady getting frustrated and less tolerant of the lady's needs. When I got to the front of the line, my approach was very different, and consequently, so was the service that I received.

Whether you are conversing with one person or a hundred people, speaking with confidence is important. After your audience (and an audience can be just one person) makes a visual assessment of you (clothing, hair, how you walk, etc.), their next assessment is almost invariably based on how you speak.

Here are a few points to consider:

- Use positive language. Seriously, nobody likes a whinger!
- Ensure you can be heard. Your audience, even if you are speaking to only a few people, should be able to clearly hear what you are saying.
- Maintain eye contact while you are speaking. Mumbling while looking for your keys in your handbag will only frustrate the person you are speaking with.
- Don't rush. Speak at a moderate pace so you can be clearly understood.
- Plan what you want to say. If you are going into a meeting then make some notes on the points you want to present. If you're going into a network meeting, joining a mothers' group or in a room with people you don't know, plan a few topics you could speak about before you get there.

Find a Confident Woman as a Role Model

We all need positive role models in our lives, so finding a confident woman you can look **over** to can be of great benefit. (I have used the word 'over' here for a reason. If you look 'up' at someone, it tends to imply you are less or lower than them). We are all amazing women in our own right - some women simply have different skills or have mastered the ones that we are inspired by. What we want to do is look **over** to them and learn from them.

So, find yourself a confident woman you can look over to, and see what they are doing. It may be a celebrity, your boss, someone in the community or a friend of yours. Even a fictitious character in a movie will work or a character modelled on a real person, like Erin Brokovich in my client's example later in this section.

When you discover a woman that you marvel at, then you want to try to pinpoint what it is that you admire about her. How does she behave? How does she walk and how does she carry herself? When you are in a situation where you feel uncomfortable or unsure, you can ask yourself 'How would my role model deal with this situation?' This can help you to approach the situation in a more confident way.

I even had one client who printed a picture of her chosen role model, made it into a bookmark and used it in her diary. This was a fabulous idea as she looked at this confident woman a number of times every day. She found it helped her to maintain her focus on being a more confident woman herself.

Confident Body Language

The body language that is required is dependent on the situation. As a confident woman, I use different body language in a management meeting or a job interview than I do having coffee with a client, lunch with a friend or shopping with my kids. My body language is different when I am in a networking meeting to when I am in a mothers' group meeting or when I am presenting on stage. Ultimately, I believe it's about being comfortable in your own skin and looking that way.

In any networking function I ever attended, I could always tell the woman who was scared out of her mind at meeting strangers because of her body language. She would always be standing on the outskirts of the group, head down, maybe focused on looking for something in her bag, shoulders slouched, trying desperately not to make eye contact with anyone. I would often make a beeline for this woman and try to talk to her and make her feel more comfortable. It is such a shame that some women feel like this.

It is easy to tell when someone with high levels of confidence walks into the room. What do they have that sets them apart from others? It is important to learn to project confident body signals, so that you appear open and comfortable with yourself. This includes the way you walk, the way you stand and any hand gestures you make.

When you are focused on increasing your confidence, maintaining the correct body language is paramount, because so much is conveyed to others based on the way you hold yourself. Here are some simple tips to help you get started:

- Stand or sit up straight and keep your shoulders relaxed. Posture helps your breathing and when you are standing or sitting up straight you can breathe effectively and reduce nervousness and anxiety. A balanced posture with your shoulders back and arms loose looks comfortable and friendly.

- Maintain direct eye contact. Look people in the eye and lean into the conversation. This shows enthusiasm and an eagerness to build rapport. Direct eye contact also indicates a level of respect and interest in what they are saying. If you find this challenging, try breaking your eye contact very briefly when laughing but remember, to concentrate on the person you are speaking with. Be interested *in* them, rather than focusing on trying to be interesting *to* them.

- Don't fidget. Standing calmly, without your feet or hands moving too much, shows that you are relaxed and comfortable.

ACT Confidently!

- Be visible. Don't hide in the corner of the meeting, sit at the back of the room or stand on the outskirts of the group. A confident woman is visible and an active part of the group or discussion.
- Walk with purpose and determination, without rushing.
- Hand gestures should be open when you start to speak as this portrays that you are being truthful.
- Don't be afraid to 'fake it until you make it'. Using self-assured body language (even when you don't feel like it) breeds a bolder self-perception that, in turn, builds confidence. Hmmm…the chicken or the egg?

When you feel yourself starting to falter, think of your favourite kick-butt confident woman and imitate what you think she would do. Imitation is a very powerful tool here, so take on the character of a confident woman and get out there!

Bad Hair Days

Yes, we have reached that stage of the book. It's all about our sexy selves; how we feel inside our skin, how we wear it and how we work it.

I know it might seem unreasonable to like your body all over; the adorable bits, the droopy bits *and* the dimply bits, but the woman wearing her bits beautifully is one of the most attractive things in the world. No exceptions. That means YOU can be one of those gorgeous glowing gals that, no matter what her assets, oozes sass-appeal. It's not about small buns, perfect boobs or little legs – never has been, never will be.

Confidence in the way you present yourself to the world is paramount – all other forms of confidence in a person are limited if this one is not present. Owning what nature gave us, accepting and not resisting our bodies, motivates us to leverage the positives and stop moaning about the imperfections.

PUMPED

Know what it's like to leave the house hoping you won't bump into anybody you know? Forget it – live on the flipside all of the time. Leaving home feeling happy with your appearance will allow you to walk with your head high, give you the confidence to face the day with enthusiasm and will put a completely different spring in your step. You will feel happier, stronger and more capable to deal with whatever comes your way, plus the added benefit is that looking as though you value yourself means other people will assume that you are capable of valuing them too.

I'm not talking about expensive clothes or extreme makeovers. Sometimes the simplest things can completely change the way you see yourself and the way the world sees you. Maybe there's a lipstick that always makes you feel good or perhaps having your nails done regularly puts you in gorgeous-mode. Avoid the pants that make you feel frumpy and the shoes that make you feel older than you are. (I don't care if they're comfortable. If they make you feel low, they're just no good!)

Louise's Story

Sometimes the world doesn't even need to see you to know that you look and feel fantastic. Louise, one of my earlier clients, was a 35-year-old mother of 2 who had taken a break from her Executive PA career 5 years earlier, when she had her first child. Since that time she had had another son and was running a home-based childcare facility where she also minded 3 other children. This worked out well for a time because she could spend the first couple of years with her own children whilst earning money looking after others.

Louise contacted me because she had decided that she now wanted to go back to her career but was concerned that her levels of confidence and motivation would not get her back into the game. The first 3 sessions went really well and Louise seemed to be moving along in leaps and bounds, getting clear about what job she wanted and re-designing her life to accommodate her new choices.

ACT Confidently!

At session 4, Louise, now being faced with the inevitable challenge of actually making contact about positions, was completely stopped. The thought of having to pick up the phone and speak to adults after so many years of speaking with children daily, terrified her. All she could think about was the fresh, bright and shiny young things that she would be up against. 'Why would anyone employ a size 16 mother of 2 who has been out of the workforce for 5 years over a petite 22 year old with a perky rack and no commitments?' she would whimper.

Over the next few weeks, we worked on changing Louise's perception about the 22 year olds and got her focusing on her strengths, her skills and the value she offered to an employer. Louise did make some phone calls about positions but they didn't go very well. She wasn't getting any interviews and her confidence was wavering again.

The next week, I asked Louise how she felt when she made phone calls like that. 'I feel like a mother and not a PA,' she said. 'I've got my tracksuit and sneakers on, I'm trying to keep the kids quiet and I can usually smell the baby vomit I inevitably have on my shoulder.'

'When was the last time you had a pair of high heels on?' I asked.

'I think I've worn flats or sneakers since my first son was born,' Louise explained. 'I have not worn a pair of pantihose or a suit jacket in over 5 years and before that I was never out of them.' My next question was a real turning point for Louise. I asked her if there was someone she admired; a confident woman that she could aspire to. Louise thought for a moment then looked at me and said 'Julia Roberts in the movie Erin Brockovich!'

In this movie, based on a true story, Julia Roberts plays a sexy, low income-earning mother who takes on the justice system with attitude and confidence. Louise immediately identified with this character and agreed to watch the movie again and get herself

PUMPED

inspired. Louise also agreed to trade in her sneakers for a pair of high heels every time she had to make a call for a prospective position. PUMPED!

At our next session, Louise turned up in a suit, pantihose and heels and was excited to tell me that she had just been for her first interview in almost 10 years. 'It worked!' she said. 'I watched the movie again and really took on who Erin Brockovich was. Then, I put the high heels on to make the calls and I felt completely different. I felt like the Executive PA again and I spoke like her too!'

Louise didn't get that first job but she was unperturbed. She had tapped into a whole new level of confidence and it was the 'Erin Brockovich persistence' (as she called it) that finally nailed her ideal job.

Red Shoes, Red Bras and All that's In-Between

My favourite colour is red. When I need to really feel incredible and get a real boost of confidence, I go straight for my favourite red shoes. It is amazing! With great red high heels on, I feel like I can take over the world! There is just something about these red shoes that puts a wiggle in my walk, a twinkle in my eye and a sense of purpose in my step. I feel strong, confident and in control. (Not bad for a $100 purchase). There are other things in my wardrobe that also give me an immediate boost, but nothing is quite as powerful as those shoes! Wearing red just seems to bring out the confidence in me.

Jan's Story

One day, I was with a client, Jan, and we were talking about techniques for increasing her confidence. Jan looked at me and said that she liked how confidently I wore red clothes and that maybe there was something in that for her. I asked Jan if she could think of anything that she would like to wear that might boost her confidence. Jan mulled this over for a moment.

'Being of a larger size,' she said, 'I don't think I would feel comfortable in bright red clothes but what I would like is new bra. One that really supports me and that will make me stand up straight.'

'What about a red bra?' I suggested.

Jan's eyes lit up. 'A red bra would be perfect.'

So that week one of Jan's tasks was to go out and find herself a new, red, supportive bra. At our very next session, Jan walked in with her head up, her shoulders back and a strut in her step. She sat down, looked me straight in the eye and then reached in under her top to reveal to me the deep red strap of her new bra.

'It's amazing' she said, 'I feel like this bra has just changed my life!'

Changed her life? I was a little amazed at the strength of that statement but hey, I knew what my red shoes could do for me so anything was possible.

'I went shopping and searched for the perfect bra. One sales assistant tried to sell me a burgundy bra but I told her that it just wasn't good enough, it needed to be red; a strong, deep, traffic light red. Finally, in the third shop I saw it. There she was, just hanging there waiting for me…a bright red supportive bra with attitude that fitted like a dream!'

I noticed that Jan was even talking differently; she carried a new air of confidence that was wafting around her.

'So,' Jan said. 'This week has been amazing! Since that purchase, I have felt like a different woman. For example, I was in the lounge room with the kids after school on Thursday and they were watching a game show on TV. I overheard the show's host talking about how you could become a contestant and I thought, why not, you only live once! I grabbed a pen and paper, wrote down the number, walked straight over to the phone and, without another thought, called the number. And guess what? I'm going to be a contestant on the show in 3 weeks' time! Can you believe that? I am just so excited - I'm definitely wearing this red bra that day!'

I was stunned and inspired. Jan, when I had first met her 5 weeks earlier was very timid and nervous about talking to anybody new because her confidence was so low. Now, here she was looking forward to appearing on national television! It doesn't get much cooler than that!

Obviously, there were a few other confidence techniques along the way but that red bra seemed to really change how Jan felt about her appearance. We experience this all the time with different outfits but do we really take note of the incredible difference an outfit can have on our confidence? There is no way I could walk into a business meeting in a pair of jeans and flats and feel the same way as I would in my suit and heels. Just the same way as I couldn't go to a gala dinner in my suit and feel as good about myself as if I were wearing an evening dress.

It is just the same when you wear sexy underwear, even if it is under your daily attire. It makes you feel sexy all day even though no one else knows. We women 'save' our nice underwear for special occasions when we want to feel good, when really, feeling good on a daily basis is what's important. We may notice how great we feel when we slip into something lacy and special or, heaven forbid a matching bra and undies set, but do we really stop to consider what it does for our confidence?

Take a moment to think about the things that you own that make you feel wonderful. Think about the little things you do differently when you wear them and aim to build those into your day…*every* day. Stop 'saving' the nice stuff for another day. Remember, it's these simple things that can make the biggest impact.

ACT Confidently!

Ladies, next time you reach for that old pair of saggy knickers with no elastic in one leg, I challenge you to think again. Hey, it could be a life-changing decision when you open that drawer. Why not reach to the back for those nice lacy knickers and bra set from the special occasion section of your drawer? That's it, the ones way in the back there; even if you're just going to the supermarket. Why shouldn't you feel great every moment that you're alive? And sure, that tracksuit is comfy but how does it really make you feel about yourself? What about in the office? My mother used to say 'you should always dress for your next position.' People treat you in a way that is relevant to the way you are presented.

So, here's what to do for an instant confidence boost:

Knickers/Panties/Briefs

Throw out all the old undies with holes, broken elastic or a saggy bum and either wear the 'good' knickers you save for special occasions today or go buy some great new knickers that feel good and hold everything in place. Sure, they can still be comfortable knickers but no more bad, dodgy, too-old-to-really-be-alive knickers allowed.

Bras

Take a good long look at your bras. Are you still wearing an old maternity bra even though your last child has just entered high school? Do you continue to wear that old comfy bra you have had for over 20 years that makes your bust line hang? I know it's comfy but it's time to go! What about the bra you continue to wear that is the wrong size, which now has your boobs bellowing over the top – just not a good look.

Take a leaf out of Jan's book and go get yourself a new, sturdy, correctly fitting bra. It can be lacy or plain and any colour of the rainbow as long as it fits, looks nice and holds you upright. You will be amazed at what a new bra can do for you!

Secret Support

Yes, yes, yes! If there are a few body parts hanging low then the multitude of secret supports that are now dangling in the lingerie sections are just for you. You'll feel great with a few more bits held into place so make these your friends.

After 2 C-sections when birthing my 'huge' babies, I have that pudgy lower section on my belly which just doesn't want to move no matter how many damn sit-ups I do. (Relax personal trainers! I know I could probably get rid of it if I did your boot camp session every morning – it's just not what I want my life to be about!) I found these wonderful shapewear skirts that go perfectly under any dress or skirt. When I am speaking in front of people or want to feel less conscious about my lower belly sticking out, I wear one and feel great. It even makes me stand up straighter too, which my physiotherapist is also happy about!

Shoes

My favourite topic – shoes! As I have said, with my red heels on I feel like I can take over the world. Have a look down at your feet. Do they need to be freshened up, maybe a good hard scrub, toenail paint and some attention? Then ensure you look after your foot fashion and wear what gives you that confident strut. If you're like most women, you probably have a great pair in the back of your wardrobe that you traded in for a pair of flats years ago. Maybe get the flat scuffs off and the heels on, for a confidence shift that will delight you! I'm not suggesting you wear 6 inch stilettos to the park, just have a look down every once in a while and check in with what you've chosen to carry you through your daily life.

This was evident to me when, after 40 years of resistance, I finally paid $40 for a pair of Havaiana thongs/flip-flops (the ones with the crystal, of course) and they have changed my life. It's not about the brand name, or the attached bling – it's all about the shift in my notion of what thongs represent. I didn't own a pair of flats until my late 20s, have never really liked thongs, and so I always looked at them with a healthy dose of preconceived negativity (there are some *really* bad ones out there). Now however, that I've found a pair that I actually like, I happily put them on and can strut my stuff in them all day long.

Virtual beauty

'Even I don't wake up looking like Cindy Crawford.'

-Cindy Crawford-

Increasingly, our standards of beauty have become unrealistic and virtually unobtainable. Judging ourselves by impossible standards and then berating ourselves endlessly for coming up short, only results in a negative self-image, perpetual disappointment and extremely low levels of confidence. We, as women, have become obsessed with comparing ourselves to the handful of genetic lottery winners that exist on the planet, and then drowning in our own sense of inadequacy! Ludicrous.

What do we think flawless thighs, an ironing board stomach and a wrinkle-free forehead are actually going to get us? Is it admiration from others (particularly those we want to attract)? Increased confidence?

Okay, well here are the facts: the looks that the standard 'beautiful' girl gets are fleeting and the things that people say about her are never solely based on her body for very long. The non-standard 'beautiful' girl who feels sexy in her own skin is infinitely more attractive to both genders - always. Think about the people you have fallen in lust and/or love with in your lifetime. How many of them have been wrapped in a perfect exterior? Take the pressure off and get real about yourself. Leverage the bits you love.

Physical attractiveness DOES NOT equal happiness or unending confidence!

Tina's Story

A few years ago I worked with Tina, a young 21-year-old woman who was a stripper. She was what I would consider to be a knockout. She had a great body, a mane of beautiful blond hair and big blue eyes. Tina turned heads on the street and had other girls wishing for her figure and her bust line – she was gorgeous!

Tina was, however, a very unhappy person. Her confidence was extremely low and, although she longed to move out of her current industry, she lacked the self-belief that told her she could do something else. As a stripper, her self-worth was completely based on how she looked, and Tina had lost all sense of her value on the inside.

Tina and I worked together for a number of months, building her confidence, exploring her alternatives and helping her to deal with an industry that was obsessed with physical appearance - but that is not why I am telling you this story. What I want you to grasp is that, even those beautiful people we admire so much for their exterior and to whom we often feel inferior to, can also be struggling with their own sense of who they are.

I'm not necessarily saying that you shouldn't lose those extra kilos or hit the gym and get into shape. Just know that until you stop the comparisons and truly accept your body for what it is your quest for happiness will go unfulfilled. It's amazing how insatiable we can be no matter what it is that we have already achieved.

Do you want people to talk about you after you've left the room in terms of 'absolutely gorgeous', 'beautiful' and 'incredibly attractive'? Want the *it*-factor? News flash: *it's* not about looks! *It's* about

ACT Confidently!

the package. *It's* about what goes on behind the eyes and what is spoken in the way you walk, talk, dress and generally present yourself. *It's* in the way you listen to others and the way you relate to yourself. *It's* how you wear what you've got and your all-important attitude to life. That's what makes an attractive woman.

Body Image

The body image debate is alive and well in the world, as we are continually bombarded with images in the media of desperately skinny women and girls – not to mention, Barbie.

When my daughter was little she played with a Barbie doll that had legs that were totally disproportionate to the rest of her body. For some reason, my daughter takes the clothes off all her dolls so I sometimes get quite a scare when I walk into the toy room and come face to face with a naked, over-perfect toy woman lying on the floor with her legs in the air!

Reports state that Barbie's legs are 50% longer than her arms although an average woman's legs are only 20% longer. Barbie would literally need to walk on all fours if she was a real woman because her legs are not proportionate to her torso. Barbie also boasts a neck that is twice as long as the average woman's and, therefore, would not be able to hold her head up without support. Her tiny body only has enough room for half a liver and a few centimetres of intestine instead of the 7.9 metres a real woman has. Her body mass index would be so low that it would be unlikely that she would menstruate or be able to have children. It is such a shame that our baby girls are being given this unachievable image of a woman from such an early age.

All magazines airbrush their photos and almost all advertising does the same. Therefore, when you are reading these magazines or seeing these advertisements you are basically comparing yourself to a cartoon. You wouldn't flick through a comic book and feel guilty that you don't have the hips of the thin, sexy illustrated woman, would you? We look at this and our brain recognises that this is a make-believe character. Well, what we all need to realise is that the women in these media promoted images should also be taken as make-believe characters. However, because these women are so lifelike, it is so much harder for our brains to accept this. Women in magazines are airbrushed, and whilst they closely mimic and resemble our reality, we need to remember that they are not real! Hard, I know, but we all need to keep working at it.

And don't get me started on social media - where every photo is filtered, enhanced and modified turning any 'real' woman into an enhanced avatar of herself. There's even a celebrity who has hired a full time person to modify her selfies before they are unleashed on the world though her social media channels! I mean, really! We're currently stuck in the selfie craze - where suddenly you go out for a quick coffee with a friend and the social media version of you comes out wrinkle-free and bright-eyed, with 3-shades whiter teeth, toned arms, tanned and 10 kilos lighter. Why do we continue to perpetuate this? Why?

There is evidence to suggest that 3 minutes of reading a magazine will make 70% of women feel depressed, guilty and ashamed. All I can say is stop it. Just Stop It! Make it a point to expose yourself to more positive, uplifting and realistic information. Recognise and appreciate that all women are equal and different at the same time. There is beauty in everyone, and whilst that beauty may not be the conventional size 8, big busted, blonde haired beauty that magazines tell us is the 'norm', it is beauty nonetheless because it is unique, unapologetic and real.

Unfortunately, it is not just in the magazines. The chance of an average woman having the same weight and height measurements as a shop mannequin is 1%. No wonder the outfit looks better in the window than it does on you in the change room.

As women in today's society, we view some 400 to 600 advertisements a day with conflicting beauty images. What we need to ensure is that we are careful about what we read and what our minds perceive to be real.

ACT Confidently!

Here are some shocking claims:

- 9 in 10 women want to change some aspect of themselves - with body weight and shape being the main concerns.
- Lower self-esteem relates to a higher desire to change one's physical self.
- The current unrealistic beauty ideals negatively influence the way a woman values her physical self and impacts her overall sense of self-worth.
- Data indicates that when a woman has a positive sense of self, she is more likely to be satisfied with her physical self and vice versa.
- A woman's self-esteem impacts her willingness to engage in life – it can be seen in her face, posture and the energy she projects to the world daily.
- Women globally allow their anxious and self-critical feelings around beauty and body image to negatively influence their engagement in a wide range of daily-life activities.

Source: Beyond Stereotypes: Rebuilding the Foundation of Beauty Beliefs – February 2006

With this information, you can see that we are all going through the same crazy process of being overly concerned about our bodies. We are all on the slippery slope of low self-worth, trying desperately to hold on. The world needs a wake-up-call in this area and there is no one more affected than us women. Think of what our kids are going to have to deal with?

Try these confidence techniques to stop the unnecessary comparisons:

1. **Appreciate YOU** - consider that someone may be looking at your accomplishments as the inspiring trailer to a life they want to lead, whilst you are hiding your achievements in amongst the

unread credits that no one pays attention to. For me, my height has always been an issue and I have often wished I wasn't quite so tall. Funnily enough, it was this exact quality that often led to me receiving the most compliments and, time and time again, I was told 'I wish I had your height.' The very thing that concerned me the most is strangely what others admired and coveted. What is it for you?

2. **Embrace YOU** – remember that there never has been (or ever will be) anyone quite like you. Embrace your uniqueness and be proud of your achievements and successes. What may seem like a small win to you, or what might not even make your radar as an achievement, for someone else may be inspiring and motivating. If you can recognise and accept this, embracing yourself will naturally follow.

3. **Compare only to YOU** – I love this quote from Albert Einstein – *'Everyone is a genius. But if you judge a fish on its ability to climb a tree, it will live its whole life believing it is stupid.'* If I'm the fish, the only thing I should be comparing myself to is my ability to swim and how well I've done that this week. As women we often aspire to certain body image ideals – we all want to look like super models, but I, for one, don't want to train, eat or work like a supermodel, so why insist on comparing my body to one? Ultimately, the best person to compare yourself to is you! The only way to measure your growth, development and personal achievements is to look back to where *you* were and see how far *you* have come. Swim as well as you can and don't be disappointed if you can't climb that tree.

4. **Love YOU or change YOU** - do you feel that your thighs are too big, your boobs are too small or your arms are too flabby? Continually complaining about these things and criticising yourself whenever you look in the mirror is totally pointless and entirely counter-productive. Love you or change you, but for goodness sake, stop bitching about you. This continuous negativity that

bounces back at you whenever you stand before a reflective surface is doing nothing to help you. It tears away at your self-confidence bit by bit, day by day. We all know that confidence comes from doing, not complaining. So… do! Don't like your thighs? Change them. Don't like your boobs or arms? Do something about it. If you can't accept it, whatever *it* is, make a committed decision to change it. The flip side is, if you're not willing to put in the work, stop whining about it. There is no in-between here. Like I said, I had issues with my height, but aside from cutting my legs off at the knees, there wasn't much I could do about it, so I've learnt to love it. The thighs however, are something I can work on, so it's up to me to do something about it.

Make Decisions

Working with a new client once, I asked her to give me an overview of what she was trying to change in her life and what, up to now, had she done about it. Unusually, the answer to this question came very easily as she detailed in length, a myriad of courses, books and classes she had done to work on her life.

As we continued to talk, I was impressed with the amount of knowledge this woman had gathered and retained. The key life areas she was focused on to change were career and work/life balance, fitness and intimate relationships and I had never met anyone who knew more or had done more work on each topic. Something didn't fit.

As our sessions continued, I watched with interest as this knowledgeable client researched more and more information. Then, it dawned on me! My client was so focused on becoming an information expert that she forgot (or resisted) putting any of this valuable knowledge into action.

So, the next session I asked her what, out of all the things she had learnt, did she want to put into practise that week? She looked at me, looked at her piles of information and then just looked at me again and sighed 'I don't know where to start. There's just too much here!'

Many people around us claim to be an expert and we rely on experts in many areas of our lives. We seek medical experts, career experts, real estate experts, and all sorts of other experts on anything from cooking to parenting. We read books, pay consultants, attend courses, watch documentaries, seek counselling, seek advice, and pay for mentoring. This is all fine but at some point, we have to recognise that we have gathered enough information and advice, and it's time to move into action. Consistently thinking you don't have enough information can become just another one of those annoying excuses that get in the way of you achieving what you want in your life!

My client, like so many of us, was so absorbed in becoming an expert by gathering information and doing every course under the sun, that she forgot the most important part – putting the information into action by making decisions. Essentially, she continued to gather information to ensure she didn't make a mistake, feeling that she needed to be an expert before attempting anything. Unfortunately, this had now become an excuse for not putting anything she had learnt into action.

Is there something that you are trying to become the expert on? Have you been putting off doing something for years because you still don't believe you know enough? Would you prefer to wait until you have all the information and all the secrets to success, before you even try? Well, I'm sorry to say that you'll never achieve success if you follow that method.

You see, information without action is useless. You can pay for all the best advice in the world but it is worthless to you if you don't do something about it.

Sometimes, we get so focused on learning from the other experts that we forget that we are the only experts in our own lives. At some point you can take all the advice and information you want, but *you* ultimately make the decisions about your life and only *you* are accountable. With

ACT Confidently!

this comes our own instinct, intuition and inner voice. Have you ever been given some advice that you just 'knew' was not correct, even though it was coming out of the mouth of a recognised 'expert'? Somehow, that specific advice just doesn't fit for us individually and we have to trust our own instinct, not everything an expert says will be right for us.

Ultimately, action is everything! Would you ever let someone in the medical profession operate on you if they have read a lot of books but never actually performed the procedure? Of course not! Always remember that you are the expert on your own life already and you have to take the information and put it into practise. *That* will be the secret to your success!

After you make the final decision - commit! Don't continually second-guess yourself. Great leaders communicate with a sense of belief in what they are doing and with positive expectations toward the achievement of their vision.

Be Self-Expressed

There is something quite inspiring about a woman who is self-expressed. Onlookers tend to envy the courage that woman has to just be herself and say or do what she wants in the moment.

Self-expression has a variety of levels so, if you have been a wall-flower for the past 20 years, then maybe volunteering to host the corporate awards night in front of 3,000 people is not such a great place to start. Maybe just start by wearing those big earrings you love or presenting a new idea to your work's sales team of 3.

As you become increasingly more comfortable with YOU, you will find it easier to just be YOU.

My favourite form of self-expression is to hit the dance floor and let go. I love to dance and at any party I am always the first on the dance floor to get things kicked off. In that moment, there are audible sighs of relief from the women lining the dance floor who are also dying to get out there - thankful sighs, that someone else has finally got it started as there was no way they were getting up first. Now they can get out there and boogie, even if it is at the back corner of the dance floor where no one can see them!

You may not ever wish to be the first person on the dance floor but if you really want to be dancing, then work on a specific confidence technique that will allow you to get out there. For you it may be about wearing that bright top that you've been hiding away in the back of your wardrobe for 2 years, waiting for the *right* time to wear it. Or, it may be about speaking to that particular person, or in front of that particular group. At the end of the day, it is your self-expression that will give you the confidence to do what you want to do. Pick a technique that works for you, that allows you to truly express yourself, and you'll find that, soon you'll be dancing wherever, speaking to whomever and wearing whatever you like. Dye your hair, wear a low-cut dress, pose for a life drawing, ride the shopping trolley back to your car, dance on the podium, laugh loudly in public or do all of the above! Having the confidence to be self-expressed will give you a freedom like no other.

Whatever you do – BE YOU! We like her best!

Set Achievable Inspiring Goals

At some time throughout any career in any industry, someone somewhere will teach you about the elaborate process of goal setting. If this hasn't been the case for you, then here is a crash course.

Firstly, it is important to look back on the year that has passed - what did you achieve? Even if it was only something small, it is important to acknowledge that accomplishment because this keeps you motivated. Have you noticed how easy it is to remember all the stuff we *didn't* achieve? And also how easy it is to forget what we *have* achieved?

ACT Confidently!

Remember that criticism doesn't work. Would you choose to be friends with someone who consistently criticised you? I hope not. So why do we allow it of ourselves?

It is then time to take a look at where you are. This is called a current reality check and it is important to be really honest with yourself! Your current reality is the foundation from where your new goals rise, so this is a necessary step in the formation of inspiring, well-structured and achievable goals.

Be honest and get real. If you're 10kg overweight, then you're 10kg overweight. If you are going backwards financially, then that's the reality. If you haven't read a book to your children in weeks, if you haven't had a date for 3 years, if you haven't done your taxes yet, then don't worry. Things can turn around, but get real about where you are on the starting blocks.

Next, look at where you are headed and, again, it is necessary to be really honest with yourself! Remember the old saying: 'If you do what you've always done, you'll get what you've always gotten'. If the road ahead sees no change in direction for you, it is highly probable that you will get the same outcome as in previous years. If there is no plan for change at this stage, you have to ask yourself whether or not a likely repeat of the outcomes of the past are what you really want. Are you truly committed to making a change?

Once you have worked through the above stages, it is then time to consider where it is you really want to go. What is it that you really want for your life? It's time to start creating the life you want and not putting it off any longer.

To make goal setting a worthwhile process we must set goals that are **workable** and, most importantly, that inspire us. A workable goal is quite specific - you know exactly what it is that you want. Not like 'to be happier' or 'to earn more money' or 'to lose weight'. Get specific! What would have to happen for you to be happier? How much more money? $5 is more – is that what you meant? How much weight? 1kg? 5kgs? 10kgs? If you don't have a specific goal, then you won't really know what you are going for and you won't recognise it when you get there.

Workable goals must also be **realistic**. There is a fine line between realistic and unrealistic; you want to stretch, but not discourage, yourself. Setting goals that are likely to be achieved with little effort will not motivate you or give you a strong sense of satisfaction. Alternatively, goals that are too hard or unachievable will de-motivate you and have you giving up easily.

You next need to set a **time frame** for your goals. I like to work with short term goals so I generally set goals that I want to achieve in the year and then break them down into a plan, focusing on 3 months at a time. My husband, however, works with a 5-year goal plan. Think about what will work for you and set the goal to be achieved within that time frame.

Now to put that **inspiring twist** onto your goal! Does losing weight really inspire you? What if your goal was to fit into that black, sexy cocktail dress you haven't worn in years or that favourite pair of pre-maternity jeans you still have in the cupboard? And instead of creating more wealth for yourself, how does 'walking through the door to your new home' strike you? The outcomes here are the same; it's just that the goals are more inspiring and invite excited focus.

Now, get a **plan** together. Think about how you are going to go about achieving this goal and get into action. Achieving what you set out to do is a great boost to your confidence so get out that notepad and get busy!

ACT Confidently!

Your PUMPED Action Plan

- If you act like a confident woman, then people will treat you as one. Fake it till you make it girlfriend!
- Look around and find that confident woman you admire – then master her moves! Imitation works. I heard about a woman once, who bought a pair of Oprah's second hand shoes so she could literally 'walk in her shoes'. She was adamant that it made a difference to her.
- Always be aware of your body language as it makes a considerable difference. Stand straight, eyes up and walk with purpose. Your physiology makes a difference to the way you think.
- Forget the bad hair days. Spending that little bit of extra effort to make yourself feel good is worth it.
- Please - don't ever wear another pair of those daggy knickers - ever! Unless you're painting the house or scrubbing the bathrooms, then maybe… but still, a big maybe!
- Remember Tina the stripper? Even she had low confidence. It ain't about your ass sister!
- Stop reading the cartoon beauty magazines. You're never going to look like them or Barbie, so keep Barbie and the mags hidden out of sight where they belong.
- Don't just read, learn or think about it… go out and do it! Remember that no amount of research or study can replace real life experiences. Make your informed decision and put that great information to work for you.
- Dance, laugh, dye your hair purple or get naked (responsibility for the law here though). Unleash your self-expression and go for it. You only live once so don't drop dead without expressing who you really are!
- It's great to have goals, but make sure they are specific to your desired outcome, close enough that you can see them but not too close that you can reach them without a bit of hard work. Most importantly, make sure they are inspiring and drive you all the way to the result you want.

Don't ever wear another pair of those daggy, bum sagging, elastic broken knickers - ever! Unless you're painting the house or scrubbing the bathrooms, then maybe... but still, a big maybe!

LIVE Confidently!

Creating an environment that supports you to live a confident life is extremely important. Motivation will waver so your environment needs to support you on a daily basis.

This section shares with you some confidence techniques to set up your environment for success!

Confidence is Catching!

'It is amazingly empowering to have the support of a strong, motivated and inspirational group of people.'

-Susan Jeffers-

Have you ever been in a room with someone who has an outrageously infectious laugh? It is almost impossible not to laugh along because the fun energy is so contagious.

Similarly, spending time with a negative person can affect you too. Have you ever listened to somebody pick fault with almost everything in their life? People, work, the weather, the government… the list is usually endless! This energy is transferable and it will always be a struggle to stay positive when you are surrounded by so much dismay and pessimism. At the very least, you'll feel angry and frustrated with the individual because they've got nothing positive to say.

Well, confidence is no different. Confident people have an energy that is magical and, thankfully, also very contagious. If you are working on building your confidence, it is vital that you spend your time with positive, uplifting and powerful people that inspire you and whose energy you are happy to 'catch'.

Take a good look at the people you currently surround yourself with. Yes, those that *you* have drawn to you. It would be acceptable to initially think that people have just turned up in your life by way of circumstance. However, you have attracted your friends in one way or another and there is a lot to be learnt from exploring the attitudes you share. Are they positive, motivated people who inspire you and bring out your best? Or do you have friends that are negative and defeated; that instil fear and doubt in you when you tell them about your goals?

Now, don't get me wrong. I'm not saying that those positive, happy, glass half-full people don't have really crappy days. Of course they do. I'm also not saying that the negative, 'life sucks' sort of people can't have a good run and have a day where they're happy to be alive. They do too – sometimes! I'm imploring you to investigate the usual mood of those people around you. If you said you wanted to start a business, climb Mt Everest or lose 10kg would they naturally fall into the category of an encourager or a discourager?

Ultimately, positive people attract positive people and negative people tend to attract other negative people. When we are feeling low and are content to look at the down-side, we are not compelled to spend time with motivated, happy people because they don't let us get away with our gripes. It is far more comforting to vent to somebody who agrees with us and provides us with further proof that we have every right to moan.

Conversely, when we are feeling strong, enthusiastic and optimistic, we have no desire to be dragged down by the pessimism of others and instead, naturally gravitate towards people that share our zest for life. See if you can identify any friends in your life that you can rely on for encouragement and positive reinforcement. Now think of anybody that you find draining to be around – and be prepared to admit that, at times, this may be the way some people find you too. A biggie, I know, but an insight like that can turn things right around!

My Encouraging Friend Story

I have a lot of positive people around me. Remember my good friend, Raquel? She is the most reliable encourager I have ever met. She has NEVER said a negative word about one of my goals, NEVER stomped on my dreams and NEVER done anything but fully support, encourage and join in the excitement of my goals - no matter how far-fetched they may have seemed at the time. She has become that person I call whenever I feel low in motivation, scared or lost. One conversation with her and I leave feeling like I can take over the world again.

As you start to focus energy on confidence building, it is important to protect your progress from the 'energy vampires' who can suck the life out of you. I strongly recommend that you distance yourself from critical people, at least until you are stronger and better equipped to deal with them. I think you would agree that we are all perfectly capable of taking our own inventory and don't need someone else pointing out errors, keeping us focused on our shortcomings or helping us to find more things to be upset about!

It is, however, also very important to take full responsibility for how these people affect you. No one can make you feel inferior without your consent. It is not what they say to you that is the issue - it is what you then say to yourself. Do you give their words credit? Do you relate to their opinion as the truth? Do you allow their negative perspective to bring you down?

It may be that you can identify a person very close to you that is not a positive influence and it would be impossible to distance yourself from them. You can still have these people in your life; you just need to be responsible for not allowing their negativity to affect you. This requires perspective, preparation, and practise.

Perspective

Throughout this book we have looked at the ways your reality is created – by what you think, what you say and the way you view the world. Your perspective is utterly unique and is shaped by a myriad of past and present factors.

If you have a perception that someone is negative or critical towards you, it is important to recognise that it is only how *you* perceive them. As soon as you decide a person is negative, all you will then tend to hear is their negativity and criticism. (Remember our earlier discussion on your 'field of reference'). Just as you tune into a particular radio station and focus your attention to it, consider that you have simply 'tuned' your listening into 'Bad Attitude FM' and now that is all you can hear.

When you can take responsibility for the station you are tuned into, you have the opportunity to then listen to what *else* the individual is saying that you may not usually hear. Is there another meaning behind the words that you may be missing?

Helen's Story

One of my clients, Helen, realised that she was really missing something. Every session Helen would raise the topic of her critical mother. Seemingly, no matter what Helen spoke to her mother about, all that came back was doubt, trepidation and criticism, which understandably, Helen took to heart. Helen was continually hurt, frustrated and annoyed with her mother and was finding her increasingly difficult to deal with. The first area we worked on was her perception.

We reflected on a time when Helen told her mother about the promotion she had been awarded at work. Helen was really proud of her achievement and was expecting support and praise, but her mother only responded with comments about the trial of extra hours and responsibility Helen would have to face. Not a hint of congratulations at all. Helen was outraged.

Firstly, I allowed Helen to say everything she needed to say about how she was feeling. In the safe environment of our session, Helen expressed all her anger, resentment and disappointment towards her mother, and really allowed herself to feel the pain. Once these emotions were acknowledged, we had a chance of seeing this incident from a different perspective.

We looked at her mother's life and her relationship to work, given that she had not been in the workforce for over 40 years. Through further discussions, Helen discovered that her mother was not given the opportunity to explore her strengths in the corporate world and, no doubt, viewed the workforce as a very difficult place for a female to be. Immediately, Helen's perspective began to change. Her mother's relationship to a job promotion was one of fear, discrimination and sacrifice and this was expressed in her conversations with her daughter.

As Helen explored this new perspective, the anger, resentment and frustration began to disappear. Yes, she was hurt that she didn't get the praise she was looking for, but she understood that her mother's view of a promotion was completely different to her own and that her lack of encouragement in this area was not due to a lack of love or pride.

Trying to find a different perspective on another person can help you to open up a different level of understanding and compassion. Why not ask yourself:

'What is this person going through in their life that has them take a negative or critical view of the world?'

Or

'Is this person being critical because they are scared and are they trying to protect me because they care about me?'

You see, how that person is reacting is rarely about you. It is all about what is going on for them and their own, unique perspective.

Preparation

Now that you have started to look for another perspective, it is important that you be prepared. You see, the problem is not that the particular individual is negative or critical; the problem is only that you have chosen to take on their negativity or criticism. Unfortunately, it's all up to you!

To prepare myself for an unpleasant environment, I have found a lot of value in the following visualisation that I encourage you to try.

The Bubble

To protect myself from negative energy, critical people or an unpleasant situation, I imagine myself inside a glass bubble. My glass bubble generally has a pink tinge to it, which keeps me calm, but you can use whatever colour works best for you. While I am inside my bubble, only positive energy can penetrate the glass (like the heat of the warm sun) and all negative energy, pessimistic attitudes or critical comments are deflected. Let them have it back - I don't want it!

Spend some time creating an image and a feeling that creates your 'bubble'. Make sure you feel strong, peaceful and happy in it. Work daily on conjuring up your bubble when you feel yourself beginning to be affected by negativity, so that you can remain untouched by it. Try it - it really works!

Practise

Like most things, this all takes practise. One day you will do well and deflect all the negativity, and the next, your resilience will waver and you will get hurt. Don't get frustrated with yourself, as this is all very natural. Just acknowledge that your resilience was low and work on building it up again. Keep practising and you will become more skilled at dealing with any negativity that comes your way.

Who is in your life that is not helping to increase your confidence? Either remove them or manage them.

Surround Yourself

If you want to be a millionaire, who should you mix with? Answer: Millionaires. Why? Because to be a millionaire you need to think, act and behave like millionaires do.

If you want to be happy, who should you mix with? Answer: Happy people, so you can think, act and behave like a happy person.

Therefore, if you want to be a confident woman, who should you be mixing with? Yes, confident women! Why? So you can learn to think, act and behave like confident women do.

Focus on surrounding yourself with people who will ensure your environment supports you with being a confident woman. Seek out some confident women role models, get mentored by a confident woman in your workplace or industry and/or go talk to the confident woman standing at the school gate when you pick up your kids. Get to know these women and find a way to get them into your life.

You have choices. If you want to be a miserable cow who is pessimistic and negative about their life, there are loads of people who you can associate with. However, if you want to be a confident woman who is strong, positive, happy and a go-getter, look for these women to have coffee with instead.

Confidence Buddy

Taking charge of your confidence levels is really important but sometimes the energy to keep ourselves in a positive, motivated and confident state of mind wavers. These shaky times are inevitable and it is important to put techniques into action to deal with these temporary moments of confidence relapse.

One of the most powerful techniques I have used to get me through these low times is the 'Confidence Buddy' technique. I have a wonderful friend who I have adopted as my Confidence Buddy and he has played an incredibly important role in my life. I call him when I stumble on hurdles, when negative thoughts begin to take over or when I am struggling with self-doubt. He can move me out of this place in one phone call and have me on my way in a completely new frame of mind.

My Confidence Buddy Story

I clearly remember one such phone call the year I attended my first National Speakers Conference. Speaking was my dream and, although I had done a few presentations here and there, going to the national conference and being amongst the best speakers in Australia was a huge thrill.

Sessions began at 1pm and by 3pm I was a blithering mess. Sitting in the conference room with 400 odd people who I considered to be much better than me was very overwhelming and when someone asked me what I speak on, the nerves, doubt, and the self-consciousness consumed me. I felt completely out of my league! With a shaky voice and a nervous tone I said, 'err…um…confidence.' At that moment, there didn't seem to be a confident bone in my body and I was less than convincing that I was worthy enough to speak on the topic of confidence!

As the doors opened onto the foyer for the first break, I ran straight past the coffee and muffin station (a first!), out to the front of the hotel and made a call to my Confidence Buddy. I knew that I couldn't stay in my own head to turn my thoughts around; I needed his strength and clarity to get me through the rest of this seemingly terrifying experience.

LIVE Confidently!

As soon as I heard his voice, tears started rolling down my face. He listened intently to the mad rush of negative thoughts that were spilling from my mouth until he had finally heard enough. I was obviously not in a life-threatening situation of any sort and in no immediate danger. All he could hear was my doubt, my fears and a whole host of exaggerated feelings that I had allowed to consume me.

Then, my Confidence Buddy went to work. 'Jodie, this is all complete rubbish,' he said. 'You are an amazing woman who inspires everyone around her. You have an amazing impact on all those that come in to contact with you and all of your presentations have been incredible. I think you should pull yourself together. This onslaught of doubt is ridiculous! You have every right to be there and you are just as good as any other person in that room. Get to the bathroom, wipe your eyes and re-do your lipstick. Then, stand up straight, walk like you mean it and get back in there! You will do just fine. Talk to people, tell them what you will be speaking about, wear a confident smile and enjoy yourself!'

And that's exactly what I did! I went to the bathroom, fixed my face, re-applied my lipstick and pulled myself together. A few quick affirmations in the mirror and I headed back into that room, walking tall. It wasn't long before a new face approached me with an outstretched hand to introduce himself. 'What do you speak on?' enquired my new acquaintance. 'Confidence for women,' I said with a strong, definite tone. 'Obviously!' came the reply.

My Confidence Buddy had saved me once again. One conversation turned a crisis of fear and doubt into a moment of power and confidence. My Confidence Buddy didn't buy into the stuff that was going on in my head and he didn't allow me to walk the path of self-depreciation. Instead, he reminded me how he saw me in the world and what it was that I was out to achieve. For that, I am forever grateful.

I really recommend you find yourself a Confidence Buddy. It is very important that you choose someone who has an attitude to life that you respect; somebody that you trust and feel completely comfortable with. This person will play a very important role in your life and they need to be up for the challenge. Now, don't fret if you can't think of anyone just now, the perfect person will turn up, I promise.

Invite that person to be your Confidence Buddy and explain exactly how you need them to support you. They cannot buy into your fears, your negative perception of a particular situation or your feelings of self-doubt. You need to be able to contact your Buddy when you are struggling with a confidence issue and know that they will be generous with their time and efforts.

The rewards for your Buddy will be immeasurable when they see the impact they are having on your life and the progress you are making. Seeing a friend take flight and being part of the process is an awesome privilege.

Your Theme Song

This is by far my favourite confidence building technique and the most fun! I have used it with almost all of my clients and I also have first-hand experience in the power of having a personal theme song.

After only a few months of running my own business, I seemed to hit a 'dip in the road' and experienced a drop in confidence and motivation. Owning my own business was something that I had always wanted to do but that didn't stop the negative thoughts pushing through, questioning whether I was skilled enough, good enough or committed enough to actually do it (remember mean old Mavis?).

I was completely over-run with these doubts when a wonderful friend of mine told me that I should find myself a theme song. I was a little cynical but, being a lover of music, I took on the task. There are many songs that represent certain times in my life but choosing one that would be my personal theme song was a much more challenging task. What was my theme? What did I want it to be about?

For 2 weeks I searched. I listened more intently to song lyrics on the radio and asked friends whether they had a theme song. I was amazed at how many people actually did, although many were relating theirs to the universal female experience of dancing around their handbag, loudly singing every word to the song 'I Will Survive'. Searching for a theme song was great fun and I found many really inspiring and motivational lyrics.

Finally, one song really resonated with me. When I heard the words to this song I felt the vertebrae in my back magically align and pull me straight. It was a song of courage and inspiration. I had found the theme song that would support me through this new business stage of my life!

'Nothing was going to stop me now.' That is my favourite line in Anastacia's song (no – not my business partner – that's just a coincidence), 'Paid My Dues'. During the next few weeks, I started my working day with the song; I would play it on the way to appointments that I was nervous about and literally recite the words in my mind whenever nasty old Mavis and her negative voice started at me. Boy, did that shut her up! I was completely astonished at how much this song could change the way I was feeling, and so quickly! It would give me courage, motivation and confidence and really kick in that powerful sensation of sheer determination that I sometimes needed. Belting it out in the shower, the kitchen and the car gave me an instant energy burst. It helped me to focus and gave me the strength to continue down the path to my dream of running my own business, no matter how hard the journey got – because 'nothing was going to stop me now!'

It may sound a little whacky, but this is a technique that works absolute wonders. Over the years I have challenged many of my clients to find themselves an anthem. Yes, they can be dubious to start with, and look at me quite strangely, but once they find an appropriate song and start building it into their Confidence Program, they too are amazed at how powerful it really can be.

Now, it is important to note: a personal theme song needs to be uplifting, inspirational and have a message that you really connect with. There are some songs that, while they give you a sense of strength, elicit that strength from a negative emotion.

Let me explain. There is many a 'getting over him' song or 'I don't need you anymore' song or 'I can do it on my own' song. These songs can be cathartic when we are dealing with a difficult situation but it will only generate strength from the wrong direction if you make one your theme. Every time you hear the song it may reignite painful memories (no matter how distant they feel) and chances are it won't inspire you to go bounding towards your dreams. Choose a theme song that draws you into the future and has you inspired about what lies ahead. One that ignites your dreams and evokes the determination to create what it is you want. It's all about *you* – not him/her or anybody else!

So, what is your theme song? I challenge you to find it. You can change your theme song whenever you like so initially just look for something that is relevant to you at this time. Find a song that you really connect with; that inspires you and makes you feel strong, motivated and confident. Then, play it every day or at a time when a quick confidence boost is necessary - this will be when you are feeling fear, doubt or negativity about something. Keep it handy and let the good times roll.

And remember - tearjerkers are out!!

Music and our Mood

Music has a very powerful influence over our mood. When we are sad, it is difficult to resist the urge to break out the slow, gooey songs from the music collection and play them one after the other.

Why do we do this to ourselves? Well, because we all like to wallow in it for a little while. Like so many other things though, it's a choice.

LIVE Confidently!

You could just as easily crawl to the stereo red-eyed and snotty-nosed and reach for the song that always gets your foot a-tappin' and your mouth a-hummin'. We could break up with the man of our dreams and play 'It's Raining Men', ready to get back out there and find another one, but we don't. We choose to wallow in the depths of depression, clutching our copy of The World's Saddest Love Songs, reciting every line.

Now, I can appreciate that there is some sense of release that can come out of this process. Just as long as you realise that you are making a conscious choice to release the pain this way and that those sad songs were not written specifically about you or your last relationship. Before I was married I had to forbid myself from listening to the old Barbara Streisand classic with the lyrics - 'You don't bring me flowers, and you don't sing me love songs.' Automatically, I become totally irrational and started seriously questioning why my boyfriend hasn't stood on a table in a crowded place and belted me out some rendition of a heartfelt love song with 4 dozen roses in his hand. Surely he can't love me?

My question is, if the music we listen to can have power over how good we feel about ourselves, and the music we listen to is a choice, why do we still choose to torment ourselves with those desperately painful lyrics when times are tough?

I would like to suggest a new revolution in music. (Don't worry I'm not going to sing!) Imagine your life if you never listened to a sad song again! That may be too much to ask, however, next time you are feeling low and you reach over for that stack of specially selected sad song lyrics, think again. Think about your options – you can choose to ride the roller coaster down or you can turn the damn thing around and head back up! Reach for the uplifting songs that make you feel great. You can still lie there on the floor and sniffle for a while, head against the speaker, wet tissue in hand; but I bet you'd be organising a bumper girls' night out a few days sooner if you trade the violins in for diva disco tunes.

PUMPED

It totally works for the kids too! In my household, we were having a run of days that started with very sleepy, unmotivated, whingy kids who didn't want to get breakfast underway, or to get ready for school. I too, was not feeling that great and was just the cranky, unfriendly mother yelling repeatedly 'get your shoes on...turn the TV off...pick up your school bag...brush your teeth...COME OOOONNNNN-NN!!!!!!!!!' Not a great way to start the day.

So, I got the kids involved and we created a playlist for our mornings. We had so much fun picking our favourite upbeat songs and pumping these out of the speakers became our new morning ritual. Wow – what a difference! We were all dancing and singing around the house as we went about our morning routine, left on time AND in a great mood! Now that's the way to start the day!

If you want to feel great and be a confident woman, get the inspirational, uplifting songs out of the collection and sing, SING LOUD!

Surround Yourself with Inspiration

It is so important that your immediate environment supports you. When you are building your confidence (or at any time, for that matter), make a conscious effort to create a world around you that is inspirational, uplifting and positive. Here are some tips that I use:

Music

Ensure that the music around you is positive and makes you feel good. Create playlists of powerful, fun and uplifting songs that you can listen to regularly. Have a morning 'Get Up and Come Alive' playlist and an 'It's Going to be a Great Day' playlist. The one I love the best is my 'Stepping Outside My Comfort Zone' playlist, which is a selection of inspirational theme songs, all with a powerful message of 'you can do it'! I always play this in the car on the way to a presentation and it really helps me to combat any nerves I am feeling.

Books

Take a good look at what you are reading and make sure this is also supporting your positive, confident outlook. I find it incredibly powerful to continue reading personal development books and inspirational biographies. These allow me to grow and continually reinforce and develop my ideas and outlook about the future, my family, my business and all other parts of my life. The inspirational biographies help me to connect with an 'I could do that too' mentality when I read about what (generally ordinary) people have achieved. I personally also love quote books and have these near my computer, on the bedside table or at strategic locations around the house. These are fabulous to just open at any page and take away a message that may be uncannily appropriate for that day.

TV/Movies

I know it can sometimes be very tempting to sit down on a lonely Friday night with a big box of chocolate and an even bigger box of tissues and watch one of those incredibly sad, bawl your eyes out, everyone dies sort of movies. And sometimes, a damn good bawl makes me feel a whole lot better, but this is not generally a good practice for someone focused on building their confidence.

My suggestion is that you really focus on what movies or TV shows you are watching and dedicate your lonely Friday night to a comedy or inspirational show instead.

There are vast amounts of evidence that prove the beneficial qualities of laughter, so a good comedy is a great place to start to change a mood from sad, dull and low to upbeat, optimistic and positive. An inspirational, feel-good story is also a great way to turn the lows into highs and some of these will even give you those bawling rights you are after.

Quotes, Affirmations and Pictures

Surround yourself with great quotes, affirmations and pictures and change them often. Stick quotes or affirmations on your fridge, your computer, next to your desk, next to your bed, on your dressing table mirror, behind the toilet door or anywhere your path crosses so you receive constant reminders to think positively. I always like to have a small but beautiful notebook in my handbag, which is full of quotes that really speak to me. It is wonderful to pull out whenever I have a spare minute or to add more quotes into when I hear a great one. I decorate it with gorgeous stickers or write in coloured pens so it is beautiful to look at and uplifts me.

A great picture can help you to imagine and focus on something you want, or to remember a really happy time. I have a picture from our honeymoon on the fridge where we are both really relaxed and immensely happy with a cocktail each in our hands. We look at this picture often to be able to remember that wonderful moment together.

Pinterest

Pinterest is my happy place! I love it. I pin loads of quotes and inspirational messages on one of my Pinterest boards. Similar to the notebook idea above, I love being able to go to these boards anytime and get inspired.

I also pin stuff that makes me happy and can turn my mood around in a few minutes. I have a board of great shoes (of course!), the myriad of things you can do with glitter, awesome stationary, funny quotes and great storage ideas.

Instagram

Instagram can also be a beautiful place to visit (if you are following the right people). Beautiful imagery can be very powerful and the subliminal messages that are fed to your brain, the more you look at these inspirational images, can have lasting and positive effects.

Instagram is also great for getting those creative juices flowing. If you feel like you're stuck on a particular project, or need a bit of creative inspiration, choose to follow people who you feel are innovative and unique. Their inspiring images may spark your own creativity and motivate you to do things you've never considered before. Achieving something new or different will always boost your confidence.

Volunteer, Donate or Help

Volunteering is good for your soul! There is a wonderful story I heard once that talked about the vegetable, fruit and herb gardens that were planted at the White House during both the World Wars. They were planted to take the pressure off the public food supply but it turned out that the gardens also provided an incredible boost to morale as people felt they were contributing something of value during tough times.

This is a great idea for all of us, as volunteering really can make incredible changes to our outlook on our own lives.

A number of years ago, I was in a place where I was really short of money, wasn't in a relationship (and really wanted one), was finding everything a bit tough and I was being a right miserable cow. I was given the opportunity to participate in a one-hour kids' show at the local Children's Hospital, which I accepted. This one hour instantly changed my outlook on life as I realised that my 'problems' were really no problem at all. In this hour I watched as small and incredibly sick children sat with big smiles in their wheelchairs or beds, tubes and monitors attached, as they watched the show. They participated as best they could with tambourines and bells and sang and laughed for the show's full hour.

In that moment, my issues melted away as I remembered how incredibly fortunate I was. In the scheme of things my personal money and relationship challenges were minuscule to the daily and hourly challenges these kids were facing. This one-hour experience made me shape up my attitude and stop focusing so much on myself. A truly invaluable lesson! Since then I have always tried to maintain some level of volunteering in my life, as I know first-hand the incredible power volunteering can have on your outlook and life.

Don't know where to start? Volunteers run many of our charities that assist countless people, both within our communities and internationally. They visit lonely elderly people, they pick up rubbish, they collect clothes and food for the less fortunate, read books to the blind, serve food to the homeless, are on committees, run events, help your local playgroup function and they even participate at your kids' school canteen.

Yes, I know you are busy but if you don't have the time or resources to be able to volunteer, there are always hundreds of great causes that are only too happy to accept all sorts of donations. Sometimes the things we take for granted or casually disregard are the very things that can be most valuable to someone else. My wardrobe is full of things I very rarely wear and I recently discovered an initiative where bras are sent to underprivileged women around the world. The bras that I donated where sitting idly in my drawers (pretty lacy items, purchased in my single and perky years) which no longer fit my post-breastfeeding boobs. It never occurred to me that it would be an unbelievable and uplifting experience for the women who would receive them. For them, my bras symbolise dignity, confidence and an opportunity to have something that we take for granted but which they would never spend money on because their primary focus must be on food and educating their children. Astoundingly, it is even considered an unnecessary indulgence for many of these women and is seen by others in their village as an unforgivable sin. Can you believe, in some places in Fiji, a woman cannot get a job unless she owns a bra? This astonishing fact only made it clearer to me that the things I take for granted can really turn another woman's life around. Perhaps you don't have time or money to give, but there's always something of value you can do if you look hard enough.

Helping someone else by volunteering, or even helping your elderly neighbour by picking up some groceries for her, can also do more than you realise for your confidence. You're not just helping them and making a contribution to others, you are also making a significant and positive change to the way you feel about yourself, which is largely due to the dopamine hit you are administering to your body. Dopamine is a hormone released into your brain, which acts as a neural transmitter to give you a natural boost of self-confidence and a general feel-good sensation, and any activity that promotes this, can only be positive.

Focus on BIG problems

In the same vain, a great way to take the focus off your self is to get some really BIG problems! Now, initially this may sound like a very strange technique but work with me here.

We can turn ourselves inside out worrying and being consumed by the 'problems' in our lives. Whether they are confidence problems, money problems, family problems, problems in your marriage, at your work, with your living arrangements or whatever, these problems tend to be on our minds a lot of the time.

What I am suggesting here is that sometimes you need to get yourself some BIG problems to worry about and then the little ones tend to pale into insignificance. Big problems like the number of homeless on the streets, the number of women living in a refuge escaping from an abusive relationship, the number of hungry children, the amount of physical and sexual abuse in our communities, the high level of mental health issues or the unbelievably high teenage suicide rates. What about saving the whales, saving the near-extinct orangutans, saving the forest or seeing the major challenges your local animal rescue office deals with. These are big problems that make our issue with finding the money for our next car payment seem not so big after all.

People who volunteer for various charities know this only too well. Yes, they may have some personal problems but, because they are a part of the solution to much bigger problems in our society, they keep their personal issues in perspective.

So, if you find you are being constantly consumed by your problems, then make an effort to find a way to be a part of our society's bigger problems and I promise you, the perspective you gain will be invaluable. You may even become grateful for the problems you do have! (Now that would be an interesting spin on things, wouldn't it?). Get yourself some gratitude attitude!

'If we threw our problems in a pile and saw everyone else's, we'd grab ours back.'

-Unknown-

Give a Compliment a Day

Another wonderful technique I have used with my clients is the 'Compliment a Day' technique. I use this when my clients seem overly absorbed with themselves, and I need to re-focus their attention on the world around them.

I say: 'Giving a compliment a day keeps the doctor away' because this small act can do wonders to change your outlook and your attitude towards a healthier mind and body.

Giving a compliment to someone can totally make their day and help you to feel good about yourself (remember that dopamine hit) – Win, Win! It also puts positive energy into the world, it makes for more smiles, it allows your recipient to feel more confident and respected and can really do wonders for your intimate relationships.

You know the old saying: What you give out, you get back. Well, you can also expect more compliments to come soaring back your way once you start this exercise, so be ready for them. Accept them graciously and allow them to feel good. People give compliments because they want to, so never dismiss this act or discount what they are saying. If they say you look great in that dress, then you do to them. Don't give them the 'oh, this old thing' line. You look good – accept it and revel in it.

Can it be that hard to give a compliment a day? No it's not, but it does take some focus as generally this doesn't come naturally to most of us. When I give my clients the task of giving a compliment a day for 2 weeks, it focuses them on this wonderful act and starts them on the path to some lasting change. Try it. It won't hurt, I promise.

Set up your Environment for Success

One of the great things about working with my business partner, Anastasia, is that we are both confident enough to be very comfortable with our weaknesses. We both know we are good (even great) at some things but at other things we stink. So knowing and accepting that allows us to set up our environment for success.

Here's a newsflash - confident women are terrible at some things! The difference is just that a confident woman does not allow her weaknesses to worry her. She affirms what she is great at and sets up an environment for success for the things she is crap at.

For example, I am terrible at spelling and punctuation and Anastasia is amazing at it. I just write, absorbed in the ideas in my head rather than the actual words on the page. I can't tell you how many times I have written a post on Facebook, only to have Anastasia text me minutes later to notify me that I have spelt something wrong. I end up deleting that post and doing it again. Not the end of the world but no doubt annoying to my faithful spelling expert. So, I build my environment for success and send Anastasia all my written work to proofread before they get published. She is dying to get her hands on this book!

I am also a highly impatient person – like really impatient! I have accepted this and know that in some areas this can be a weakness. Do I care? No! I have accepted that I am highly impatient and acknowledge that this can cause problems (especially for my husband) so I have set up systems to deal with this. For example, I have absolutely no patience for trying to find a parking spot at a shopping centre. I cannot stand driving around and around. I become highly frustrated, end up with parking rage and usually scream at the kids as I fight for a spot. Not a very successful way to run my life! So, to be successful in this area, I only go to a shopping centre at the very minute the doors open. This way I get a parking spot straight away, can usually park where I want and I don't have all the frustrations and aggression that come with my impatience for looking for parking. Problem solved!

I also hate cooking. I have no creativity in this area; I don't care if I eat the same thing every night. If the meal isn't ready in 10 minutes, then it's just taking too long. When I got married and had kids this approach didn't work, so I needed to focus some energy on finding a system that supports me in this area and allows mealtime to be a success in our home. Now I know that I need to write a weekly meal plan, have a folder full of quick recipes that work for me and I also subscribe to a recipe magazine to give me new ideas. Yes, I still hate cooking and I'm a very long way from 'Masterchef' but my system supports me to get some decent, quick meals on my family's table without all the stress.

If you are terrible at time management then get a time management system, a good diary, or a secretary and let them manage your diary.

If you are a terrible cleaner then don't clean. Get a cleaner in.

If you are terrible at remembering birthdays, don't beat yourself up. There are websites and apps now where you can load in all the important birthdays and anniversaries and they will automatically send you an email or notification when it is coming up.

LIVE Confidently!

Your PUMPED Action Plan

- Confidence is contagious – surround yourself with attitudes you admire and people who believe in you.
- Consider the people in your life and note those that drain your energy – take full responsibility for the way they make you feel and act accordingly.
- Perspective - challenge the way you listen to the negative people around you and put yourself in their shoes for a moment. You may discover a reason for their bad attitude which can help you release your frustration and reach acceptance.
- Preparation - create a powerful visualisation that helps you preserve confidence and optimism in a difficult environment.
- Practise - be kind to yourself. There will be days when you will be great at holding your head high when the energy vampires are biting and other days you'll let them suck the blood right out of you. Keep practising to become a master.
- You have choices! Kick the miserable acquaintances out of your life and surround yourself with positive, confident women.
- Enrol, bribe or pay for a Confidence Buddy. Someone who will help you out of the low moments of a confidence crisis.
- Find yourself an awesome theme song and play it loud!
- Ensure you are surrounded by all things positive and inspiring. Get great books to read, make a perfect playlist and have a regular big belly laugh to a great comedy and pin up great motivational quotes everywhere.
- Go and volunteer, donate or help! It will change the lives of others and give you that well-deserved dopamine hit.
- Get yourself a big problem. Our world has many big problems that need your help. You'll get the perspective and gratitude attitude you just might need.

- Give a compliment a day – every day. Yes, even to strangers.
- Create an environment for success - Who cares that you are terrible at doing certain things? Confident women accept their weaknesses, put systems into place to deal with them and simply sort it out!
- Smile – you are on your way to living life in the power lane! Life which is happier, the journey options are endless and there are no cul-de-sacs to speak of. The ultimate road trip!
- Smile – you are on your way to living life in the power lane! A life which is happier, where the journey options are endless and where there are no cul-de-sacs to speak of. The ultimate road trip!

Confidence and belief in yourself are the most important life lessons you can master.
Be YOU!
We like her best!

The Dream

It is Monday morning on a crisp winter's day sometime in the future and you are sitting on a bench at the edge of a busy walkway. All sorts of people are walking by; some on their way to something, others on their way from something and some just out for a stroll. For such a frosty morning, you are surprised at the energy you can sense in the air. It is as though there is a warm effervescence wafting through the street and you're not sure what to make of it until you look a little more closely at the women passing by.

Each woman is walking with a serene smile behind her eyes, holding her body with affection and pride; not rushing, but stepping each pace with purpose and joy. You catch many of them acknowledging each other in delight; some silently, others with enthusiasm. Every one of these women looks incredible whether she is young or old, big or small. There is a sparkle in their appearance and a knowing in their faces.

One woman is humming a sassy tune as she passes and smiles as she notices the vixen-red heels on another passer-by. You snatch a glimpse of an ornate and gorgeous bra strap on a big beautiful mama as she hails a taxi with a wink and a grin. It's funny, you think, that she should be wearing her best underwear on a day like today – but she looks amazing.

Two women with prams are walking together and laughing. As they pass, you hear one of them say, 'It was the most incredible thing anyone has ever said to me – so it went straight into my WOW book! Today I'm feeling like a million dollars.' You smile to yourself. The confidence is oozing out of her.

PUMPED

As you sit and contemplate the dynamics around you, you begin to get the sense that all of these women have a wonderful peace about them; as though they are entirely ready to take on absolutely anything that life may throw at them.

You notice too, that each woman has her own 'flavour'. It is as if you can see the essence of them just by looking their way. It appears as though each of them has climbed inside themselves, taken note of every unique characteristic and stamped that spirit all over her outside. What grips you the most about this, is that there is not one woman that is more beautiful than any other. Each flavour is utterly delectable in its own way.

Watching these women, you realise you can't imagine any of them at the mercy of anything or anyone; that they are actively choosing their own destiny. It makes you feel empowered just seeing that! You also can't imagine any of these women subjecting anybody to criticism, blame or gossip. It is as though the energy you are breathing in is actually compassion radiating from these women.

All of a sudden you sit up straight with shock. You've just noticed something extraordinary! Not one woman is comparing herself to any others! You check and double-check. Nope, there is not a whiff of that tell-tale look of despair you know so well. But how can this be? Are all these women so secure in themselves that they are not tempted to think, 'I wish I had…'? You look again just to be sure. Unbelievable. The contentment in the air is unmistakeable.

It strikes you that although these women are all incredibly magnetic; none of them are by any means 'perfect'. It occurs to you that there is no concept of perfection here. The only standards they are working by are their own. Your desire to live in this place and feel like these women do is overtaking you. You wonder why women torture themselves so much where you come from if this is what is on the other side? This feels like a kind of heaven!

The Dream

A group of schoolgirls collect around your bench and you immediately notice the lack of self-consciousness in all of them. They are casually discussing their classes and you raise an eyebrow when they mention self-esteem and confidence sessions. You are amazed that they teach such subjects in schools.

Two of the older girls are chatting about their future plans and you are impressed to hear them talk about wonderfully inspiring possibilities for each other. It seems they have been inspired by the role-models in their lives. Now the world is their oyster and they're thoroughly excited at the prospect of cracking the whole thing open to jump right in! They know they will face fear but they also know that fear is a natural part of life and not something to back away from.

Some schoolboys stop by briefly to talk to the girls and you are astonished at the respect they display as they all walk off together. 'This is not the way it worked when I was at school!' you scoff to yourself.

Suddenly, through the midst of the pedestrians appears a jogger. As she passes each person you see their faces light up. She is just as captivating as every other woman you have seen this morning, but you're not sure why she is getting quite so much warmth from everybody. Then, she jogs past you and you see why. She's singing her theme song aloud to herself as she runs through the crowd. She doesn't have a care in the world. Awesome! Full self-expression.

Your attention switches back to the crowds in front of you, men and women alike, and out of nowhere a question pops into your head, 'Everybody just seems so content. Have none of these people been struck by tragedy; have they not done things that they wished they hadn't done? Why does it feel as though all these lives are so damn good?'

Your brow is creased in contemplation when a woman takes rest beside you. She smiles a generous and loving smile so you start talking. Soon you are asking her the very questions you had asked yourself and the answer comes back very clear. 'You won't find guilt here. You won't find regrets. The past is acknowledged, of course, but it is the lessons that are learnt and taken with us through our lives, not the ghosts of events gone by.'

'I need to get my friends and family to this place as soon as possible! I need my daughter to grow up in a world like this.' you say. The woman giggles as she stands to leave. 'You can begin to create this for yourself and the people around you right now, if you like.'

You begin to feel a determination forming like concrete down your spine.

'This could be my life?' you question. 'Could I really feel as wonderful as these women I see?'

'Of course,' the woman says. 'It's all inside of you already. Just do what it takes to be the amazing woman you already are. Accept her, love her and show her to the world. Be a confident woman and you will begin to RISE.'

My attitude of gratitude!

This book has been through so many phases of my life, over so many years, and there are just so many people who provided me with love, encouragement and positive words. My deepest thanks to them all. Every one of you kept me going!

I'm always truly thankful for Janelle (my life-long mentor), Liz (who helped make my words shine), Melissa, Melanie, Kerry, Therese, Lauren, Kate, Karen, Rakia, Kendra, Barbara and all the other exceptional friends who gave me the 'you can do this' speech or a right royal kick up the butt – whichever was needed at the time!

A massive thank you to all my family for their love and support. Sincere gratitude to Aunty Pauline who gave me so much support with the kids. It's invaluable to have someone to mind your kids, who loves and cares for them as much as you do.

A heartfelt thanks to Rhonda MacKay, my fabulous editor, for your invaluable guidance and advice. SO glad I found you!

Kelvyn – my long-time friend and confidence buddy! Your guidance always changes my life for the better. You always believed in me and this book, and the first copy is yours! You are the best at stopping the doubt in my head.

Raquel – seriously girlfriend – you are freaking amazing! You never, ever, once allowed me to think small or give up. You shine a bright, sparkly light of positivity, inspiration and motivation for me and every other woman around you that we can't help but follow. What an amazing world we would live in if every woman alive had a friend like you!

My attitude of gratitude!

Anastasia – my extraordinary business partner. You've spent hours editing, giving this book your love, fixing all my punctuation and spelling and believing in its success. You took this manuscript off the shelf and brought it back to life. You bought me back to life too! You believed in me and my dream, and simply said 'Let's do this'. You got us here and for that I am forever grateful.

I started this book before I was married with children but starting a book and finishing a book are two very different things. Thank you to my husband, Dave, who believed in his girlfriend when she said she wanted to write a book and then continued to encourage his wife to 'back herself' and keep going. My deepest love and gratitude is for you!

To my two beautiful children – what amazing inspirations you are! I see in you all the love, self-expression and confidence that I hope you can keep forever. Let's hope Mumma can join the many others to make a big enough change in the world to allow that to happen.

And, of course, to you – the reader. I hope you found here what you were looking for. Remember, you just need to click those red, sparkly heels as you have had the confidence inside you all along. Show us You!

About RiSe Women

RiSe Women has a big vision – Confident Women Globally. A vision that every woman on the globe has the right to be confident. They deserve love, dignity and the right to be heard. They deserve to be, and love, who they are!

RiSe Women is committed to making a difference to women throughout the world by guiding them, inspiring them and supporting them to have the confidence levels they have always dreamed of. They offer inspiration and practical tips through their blog, e-books and social media plus coaching and programs for individuals who want a more personalised approach.

For more inspiration, programs, e-books and resources go to www.RiseWomen.com

Speaking Opportunities

Jodie is available for speaking opportunities – her key message being 'you can create the confidence levels you want'.

Her presentations are highly engaging with practical tools that ensure the audience is motivated and inspired throughout. Her humour, wit, inspiring stories and amazing insights make her instantly relevant and relatable to all audiences and keep the presentations light and entertaining.

Jodie is authentic, real and extremely passionate about her subject, which comes across in all her presentations. She is very approachable which allows her audience to feel comfortable and at ease.

With a background in event management, Jodie knows how to ensure your event is a success and that your specific objectives are achieved.

For more information contact us at **info@risewomen.com**.

Permissions

Brian Tracy - Brian Tracy is Chairman and CEO of Brian Tracy International, a company specializing in the training and development of individuals and organizations. Brian's goal is to help people achieve their personal and business goals faster and easier than they ever imagined. Brian Tracy has consulted for more than 1,000 companies and addressed more than 5,000,000 people in 5,000 talks and seminars throughout the US, Canada and 55 other countries worldwide. As a Keynote speaker and seminar leader, he addresses more than 250,000 people each year. For more information on Brian Tracy programs, go to: www.briantracy.com

Susan Jeffers - Susan Jeffers, Ph.D. author of Feel the Fear and Do It Anyway®. www.susanjeffers.com

Eleanor Roosevelt - *You Learn by Living: Eleven Keys for a more Fulfilling Life [1960]*

www.ingramcontent.com/pod-product-compliance
Lightning Source LLC
Chambersburg PA
CBHW050532300426
44113CB00012B/2066